W.I.N.O.S.™

(WOMEN IN NEED OF SANITY)

COOK WITH WINE

By: Bonnie Jesseph

www.WinosHaveFun.com
www.WinosBuddies.com

W.I.N.O.S.™ Standard Abbreviations

tsp.	=	teaspoon	sm.	=	small
T.	=	tablespoon	med.	=	medium
c.	=	cup	lg.	=	large
oz.	=	ounce(s)	pl.	=	pint
lb.	=	pound(s)	ql.	=	quart
sq.	=	square	doz.	=	dozen
ctn.	=	carton or container	bu.	=	bushel
pkg.	=	package(s)	env.	=	envelope(s)
btl.	=	bottle(s)	pkl.	=	packet(s)
liter	=	liter	mg.	=	milligram(s)
approx.	=	approximately	gm.	=	gram(s)
temp.	=	temperature	gal.	=	gallon(s)

OTHER W.I.N.O.S.™ COOKBOOKS

W.I.N.O.S. ™ HORMONAL MOMENTS (Cooking with Wine and Chocolate)
MAN YOUR GRILL Cookin' & Grillin' With Beer
W.I.N.O.S. ™ GO TAPAS, Appe-teasers and Mini Meals
W.I.N.O.S. ™ (Women In Need of Spirits)

Cover Design By:
Sandy Johnson

First Printing - July 2006
Second Printing - November 2006
Third Printing - February 2007
Fourth Printing - August 2007
Fifth Printing - December 2007
Sixth Printing - May 2008
Seventh Printing - January 2009
Eighth Printing - October 2009
Ninth Printing - February 2011
Tenth Printing - March 2012

ISBN # 1-57166-453-X

© Copyright 2006
First through Ninth editions printed in U.S.A. Tenth edition printed in China.

Making a difference with every sip.®

<u>What is it</u>?

A club for fun loving women (and men) who enjoy food, wine, laughter and getting together for a little "sanity" in their lives, all while giving back and leaving a legacy!

<u>Member Benefits</u>:

Your membership will include:
- Social events such as winery tours, wine tastings, luncheons, shopping, etc.
- On-line newsletter with recipes and wine pairings
- Advice from wine "experts"
- Ideas for entertaining, dinner menus, cocktail parties, girlfriend night "ins"
- Access to WINOS MOMENTS™ - funny quotes and stories to get you through the day, like "what made you want to drink today"!
- Discounts on products from www.winoshavefun.com
- How to start a local WINOS BUDDIES CLUB™ in your area
- Annual meetings, cruises and much, much, more...

<u>Leaving a legacy</u>:

A percentage of every membership will be donated to various worthy causes through your local chapter and on a national level.

SEE OUR WEBSITE FOR MORE DETAILS! www.winoshavefun.com
www.winosbuddies.com

Dedication

For our 25th wedding anniversary, I dedicate this book to my great, very patient and supportive husband who has eaten just about every morsel I put in front of him and cleaned up after my endless kitchen messes. Here's to many more family dinners, cocktail parties, buffets, dinners with friends and future gastronomic concoctions. May 2006.

A special thank you to our children, Jason, Lane, Bethany and Blaire, who have survived my culinary experiments for the past 25 years and are still alive today to tell all the horrifying stories.

A special thank you to my big brother, Scott, and two younger sisters, Susie and Jan, who have stuck by me, helped provide recipes, laughter and a whole lot of ribbing along the way.

And finally, a heartfelt thanks to a very talented young woman, Sandy Johnson, who designed the front and back covers of this book in record time.

Forward

This book was a group effort, including the name. W.I.N.O.S.™

Women in Need of Sanity (my sister, Jan's, idea, and it stuck)
Women in Need of Sex (my husband's idea, typical! Good Lord, do they ever think of anything else? Oh yeah, I forgot. Golf and Food! HaHa.)
Women in Need of Something, but can't remember what! (uh, that would be me)

I am not a chef by any stretch, just a foodie who happens to like to drink wine, cook and entertain family and friends. A special thank you goes to all my family and friends who volunteered recipes and to be guinea pigs over the years and who subjected themselves to my culinary delights and disasters. Of course, the kids will tell you they never volunteered for the assignment of taste testing and love to tell that they always knew when dinner was ready because the smoke alarm went off. Brats! The darn thing did go off just once; but what moron builder would put a smoke alarm directly above the cook top? Just how dumb is that! Geez. And, of course, there was the time I accidentally burned a hole through my very first Betty Crocker Cookbook. (It wasn't my fault the burner turned itself on right beneath it.)

As a wife, mother, full-time stepmother, businesswoman, volunteer, student, caregiver and now a grandmother, I learned to cook through trial and error. As one son said, "Mom, HOW MUCH are we having for dinner?" There were times when our food bill was higher than our mortgage! I hated to cook every night and nicknamed the dinner hour as "arsenic hour", until I discovered wine. I started adding wine to my concoctions and even though the alcohol burns off, the taste of it enhanced the dish. Psychologically, wine helped me make it through all the rushed dinners, so we could get to boy scout meetings, soccer practice, football, basketball, track, swimming, lacrosse, ballet, piano, guitar lessons and whatever else our kids signed us up for. (And to think my husband thinks W.I.N.O.S.™ should stand for Women in Need of Sex. Just where are we supposed to fit THAT into our lives?)

Even if your dinner does not turn out perfect, just remember that the greatest honor you can bestow on anyone is to invite them into your home. Slap a glass of wine or drink in their hand, and they will be happy. If you burn the dinner, give them lots of wine, and they won't even remember! Now with so many good wines at $10 and under, you can get them happy fairly inexpensively. If they are someone you don't like or they turn into a jerk, give them my enemy specialty: Barbecued Road Kill with Ex-lax Gravy.

Enjoy,
Bonnie Jesseph

Guidelines for Use of Wine

🍇 If you come across a recipe that doesn't call for wine or sherry, and you would like to add it, follow this guideline:

1 tablespoon of wine per cup of sauce or soup.
1/4 cup wine to season braised meats for four people.
1/2 cup wine for a beef stew.

🍇 As much as 2 cups wine for a marinade or to baste a ham or a roast during cooking.

🍇 You don't have to use expensive wines in your recipes. But please, get rid of any cooking wine or inexpensive cooking sherry in your pantry. If you wouldn't drink it, don't put it in your food.

🍇 Remember, the alcohol from wine or any liquor burns off while cooking. Your recipes will be safe to serve to children or non-wino guests. It's all in the flavor.

Have fun and experiment!

Last Minute Tricks

🍇 Try Vermouth for a chicken marinade or basting sauce. You'll have everybody guessing.

🍇 Moisten stuffings with equal parts broth and table wine.

🍇 For ham or corned beef: prepared mustard, thinned with white wine.
Or try something hotter - dry mustard mixed to a paste with wine.

🍇 Glamour treatment for vegetables: frozen, cooked, or canned artichoke hearts in cream sauce with white wine replacing some of the milk. Buttered crumb topping. Broil until bubbly. Try it on asparagus, too.

Reasons To Drink Wine

1. It's good for your heart, according to someone.
2. Because you don't like beer.
3. It makes ugly guys look better by the end of the night. (Courtesy of my daughters.)
4. You've gained weight. One glass won't hurt you!
5. You've lost weight. Celebrate!
6. You didn't get the promotion you wanted. Those idiots!
7. You got the promotion you deserved. They finally got smart.
8. You didn't get the job you wanted. Go for another one.
9. You got the job you wanted. You go girl!
10. You broke up with your boyfriend. Set your sights higher.
11. Your boyfriend broke up with you. His loss!
12. You broke up with your girlfriend. Set your sights higher.
13. Your girlfriend broke up with you. Her loss!
14. You passed an exam. Good for you!
15. You ran out of money. Must be the price of gas!
16. You just finished the last load of laundry. Take a load off, sit and drink!
17. Your son/daughter won the game. Cool beans!
18. You broke a nail. Don't you just hate when that happens?
19. You had a great day of golf. For me, this would be a miracle.
20. You had a bad day of golf. Define bad.
21. You are on Weight Watchers, and a glass of wine is only 2 points. Yea!
22. It's cheaper than therapy.
23. You want to kill someone and drinking wine is cheaper than hiring a lawyer.
24. You are a lawyer. Sorry.
25. You became a grandmother. Congrats!
26. You got married. You will definitely need wine!
27. You got divorced. Remember, a really bad relationship is not better than no relationship.
28. Your ex isn't happy. Living well and being happy is the best revenge.
29. Maybe it's true that life begins at fifty...but everything else starts to wear out, fall out and spread out. Might as well have a drink.
30. Because it tastes good and makes food taste even better!

Drink and cook responsibly. -BJ

Notes & Recipes

_____

_____

_____

_____

_____

_____

_____

_____

_____

_____

_____

_____

_____

_____

Table of Contents

APPETIZERS 1-24

VEGGIES & SALADS 25-50

SEAFOOD 51-88

POULTRY 89-124

MEATS
    BEEF-PORK-LAMB 125-170

SOUPS, STEWS, SAUCES,
    MARINADES & MISCELLANEOUS 171-194

DESSERTS 195-216

INDEX 217-224

METRIC CONVERSION CHART 225

FAVORITE RECIPES
FROM MY COOKBOOK

Recipe Name	Page Number

Appetizers

FAVORITE RECIPES
FROM MY COOKBOOK

Recipe Name	Page Number

🍷 Hot Crab Souffle

6 to 8 servings

8 to 12 oz. imitation crab, flaked
1 T. fresh lemon juice
1 or 1 1/4 c. finely-chopped celery
2 T. grated onion
3 T. cream sherry ☺
3 eggs, beaten

2 T. chopped green pepper
1 c. mayonnaise
1 c. seasoned croutons, crushed
1/2 to 1 c. shredded Cheddar
    cheese

Preheat oven to 350°. Grease quiche dish. Mix crabmeat, lemon juice, celery, onion, sherry, eggs, green pepper and mayonnaise. Pour into prepared pan. Mix croutons and Cheddar cheese; sprinkle on top.
Bake for 25 minutes, or until knife inserted in center comes out clean.
Note: If using a pie crust, bake at 400°.

🍷 Hot Crabmeat Dip

1/2 lb. processed American cheese
1/2 c. butter or margarine

1 (7 1/2 oz.) can crabmeat
Sherry ☺

Melt cheese and butter in top of double boiler. Stir hard until blended. Mix in drained crabmeat and enough sherry to give spreading consistency.
Note: Serve in chafing dish with crackers.

1

Sherried Tuna Pimiento Dip

About 2 cups

1 (4 1/2 oz.) can pimientos, drained
  & ground or chopped
2 (3 oz.) pkg. cream cheese,
  mashed
1 (6 1/2 to 7 oz.) can tuna

1/3 c. sherry ☺
2 T. mayonnaise
1 tsp. grated onion
1/2 tsp. Worcestershire sauce
Salt, pepper & garlic salt

Combine ingredients and whip in your mixer or blender. Heap into a bowl and keep cold until 1/2 hour before you wish to serve. Accompany with potato chips, crackers or melba toast.

Pickled Shrimp

12 servings

1 1/4 c. dry white wine ☺
1/2 c. salad oil
1/4 c. garlic vinegar
1 tsp. seasoned salt
1/2 tsp. dried dill weed

4 drops Tabasco
Dash of Jamaica allspice
6 c. lg. cooked, cooled, shelled
  shrimp

Mix first 7 ingredients. Pour over shrimp. Refrigerate several hours, or overnight.

Crab and Salmon Ring

6 to 8 servings

4 pomegranates
2 pkg. (2 T.) unflavored gelatin
7 T. dry white wine ☺
2 T. fresh lemon juice
1 lb. salmon fillet, cooked &
  flaked, all bones removed
1 lb. cooked crabmeat, picked
  over, all cartilage removed

1 c. finely-ground blanched
  almonds
2 c. milk
Salt & white pepper, to taste
Radishes & tender beet greens, for
  garnish (opt.)

Working with one at a time, break each pomegranate open in a bowl of cold water and remove the seeds from the honeycomb interior (they should float to the top of the water). In a sieve, rinse and drain the seeds. Set aside. Repeat with remaining pomegranates.

In a small heatproof bowl, combine the gelatin with the white wine and lemon juice and let soften for 10 minutes. Set the bowl of gelatin in a pan of hot water and let stand, stirring occasionally, until completely dissolved.

In a food processor, combine the salmon, crab and almonds; purée until smooth. With the motor running, add the milk in a stream and continue to purée just until combined well. Transfer to a bowl, stir in the gelatin, 3 tablespoons of the pomegranate seeds. Salt and pepper to taste. Reserve the remaining pomegranate seeds for garnish.

Rinse a 6 1/2-cup ring mold with cold water. Do not dry. Pour the fish mousse into the mold, smoothing the top. Cover with plastic wrap and chill for 3 hours, or overnight.

To serve: Dip the mold up to its rim in hot water for 30 seconds. Run a thin knife inside the mold to loosen the mousse and cover mold with an inverted plate. Invert mousse onto plate, and garnish with the reserved pomegranate seeds, radishes and beet greens.

3

Stuffed Clams

8 servings

24 cherrystone clams
1 c. dry white wine ☺
1/4 c. water
1/2 tsp. salt
3 T. olive oil
1/2 c. chopped onion
1/2 c. long-grain rice

1/4 tsp. pepper
1/2 tsp. allspice
1/4 tsp. cinnamon
3 T. currants
3 T. pine nuts
2 T. chopped parsley

Wash and scrub clams well, discarding any that are open. Place clams in a large pot with wine, water and salt. Cover and steam for 10 minutes, until shells open; drain and discard any that have not opened. Cool and remove clams from shells; reserve shells. Strain pan juices and reserve.

Sauté onion in oil until golden. Add rice and 1 cup strained juice; bring to a boil. Cover and reduce heat to low; cook for 15 minutes. Add peppers, spices, currants, pine nuts and parsley to saucepan; simmer 5 minutes. Remove from heat and let cool. Dice the clams and add to rice mixture. Stuff shells with mixture. Refrigerate until well chilled, then serve.

"All stressed out and no one to choke?" --Unknown
(Drink wine!) BJ

 Holiday Cheese Bowl

About 1 3/4 cup

Your guests will ask for this recipe!

2/3 c. Sauterne, Chablis or other white dinner wine ☺
1 T. instant minced onion
3/4 tsp. powdered sage
1/2 tsp. dry mustard

Pinch of black pepper
1/2 lb. Cheddar cheese
1/4 lb. blue cheese
2 T. toasted sesame seeds

Combine wine, onion and spices. Let stand about 10 minutes. Crumble cheeses into mixing bowl. Beat in wine mixture until thoroughly blended. Heap into serving bowl and sprinkle with toasted sesame seeds. Spread may be stored, covered, in refrigerator until ready to use, or frozen if long storage is necessary.

Variation: For a soft cheese dip, add 1/2 pint (1 cup) sour cream and seasoned salt to taste to above recipe. Makes about 2 1/2 cups dip.

"When I read about the evils of drinking, I gave up reading."
--Paul Hornung

Brie and Bourbon

About 12 servings

1 (2 lb.) round of ripe Brie
2/3 to 1 c. bourbon ☺
1/2 c. brown sugar

1/2 c. pecans, chopped
Crackers

Combine bourbon, brown sugar and chopped pecans. Carefully cut off the top rind of the Brie.

To serve: Place Brie in ovenproof serving dish. Pour bourbon mixture over the Brie. Bake at 350° for 15 to 20 minutes. Serve hot with your favorite crackers.

Stuffed Edam Cheese

1 (7 to 8 oz.) Edam cheese
1/4 c. butter
1/2 tsp. dry mustard
Dash of Tabasco

1/4 c. chopped green olives
2 tsp. minced dehydrated onion
2 to 3 tsp. dry wine ☺
2 tsp. caraway seed

Cut top from Edam cheese. Scoop out inside and blend with remaining ingredients. Pack back into shell.

Serve: With crackers or icebox rye. The red wax shell makes a colorful container. No dish to wash.

Note: For easier handling, remove cellophane while cheese is cold. Leave at room temperature for several hours before trying to scoop cheese out of wax shell.

6

Chutney Party Pinwheels

36 servings

2 (8 oz.) pkg. Neufchatel cheese,
  softened
4 oz. Cheddar cheese or English
  Cheshire, shredded
2 scallions, minced
1 T. curry powder

1/2 c. diced celery
1/4 tsp. salt
5 T. dry sherry ☺
4 (12") tortillas
Chutney, chopped

In a bowl, combine Neufchatel, Cheddar cheese, scallions, curry, celery, salt and sherry. Mix well. Spread even layer on tortillas. Top with a thin layer of chutney. Roll up, jellyroll fashion, and wrap tightly in plastic wrap. Chill at least 2 hours.

Serve: When ready to serve, cut off ends and cut rolls into 1-inch slices.

"Warning: I have an attitude, and I know how to use it."
--Unknown

7

♓ Crab Puffs

Makes 4 dozen

You can fix these party goodies a day early, keep them chilled, then just heat at 350° and serve.

2 pkg. pie crust mix
1/2 clove garlic, minced
1 T. finely-chopped onion
3 T. butter
1/4 c. flour
1 3/4 c. cream
1/2 tsp. salt
1/3 c. sherry or Madeira ☺
Tabasco sauce

1 (6 1/2 oz.) can crabmeat, flaked
1 c. grated sharp process cheese
1 (8 oz.) pkg. cream cheese
1 tsp. Worcestershire sauce
1/4 c. cream
1 tsp. paprika
1 tsp. dry mustard
1 egg

Prepare pastry as directed on package, rolling it to 1/8 inch in thickness. Cut pastry with fluted 1 1/2-inch round cookie cutter. Press rounds into tiny muffin pans, making sure crust covers bottom and sides of cups. Prick pastry, then bake at 425° for 8 to 10 minutes, or until lightly browned. Cool. Sauté garlic and onion in butter until lightly browned; blend in flour and gradually add cream, stirring over moderate heat until mixture is smooth and thickened. Stir in salt, sherry, drop or two of Tabasco, and crab, mixing well. Spoon into pastry shells. Mix cheese, Worcestershire sauce and cream until fluffy; then mix in paprika, mustard and egg. Spread over top of crab-filled cases and broil until puffed and lightly browned, 3 to 4 minutes.

 Shrimp Bake

10 to 12 servings

3 lb. boiled shrimp, shelled &
  cleaned
1 tsp. salt
1 clove garlic, minced
3/4 c. butter

1 c. bread crumbs
1/2 tsp. pepper
1/2 tsp. paprika
Dash of cayenne
1/2 c. sherry ☺

Combine all ingredients, except shrimp. Blend well. Place alternate layers of shrimp and crumb mixture in a bake-and-serve dish, or in 12 individual shells. Last layer should be crumbs. Bake at 400° to heat through.

Note: The baking time will depend on the size of the container and the temperature of food when it is placed in oven. It is important that it be piping hot, but not dried out. Individual shells at room temperature may be hot in as little as 8 to 10 minutes. A single container will require around 25 minutes to heat through.

"Of course I don't look busy... I did it right the first time."
--Unknown

♀ Shrimp Supreme

1 (12 oz.) pkg. frozen shrimp
1 onion, chopped
1/3 green pepper, diced
2 T. butter
2/3 c. dry sherry or vermouth ☺

1/2 c. cream of mushroom soup,
  undiluted
Salt, pepper, garlic salt, to taste
1 jar sliced pimiento
1/2 c. grated sharp Cheddar cheese
1/3 c. bread crumbs

Cook shrimp according to directions on package. Sauté onion and green pepper in butter. Add sherry or vermouth. Simmer until liquid is almost evaporated. Add soup, seasonings, pimiento and cooked shrimp. Put in casserole. Cover with grated Cheddar and bread crumbs. Bake at 325° for 20 to 30 minutes, until warmed through. Place under broiler until slightly browned.

♀ Sesame Chicken Kabobs

10 servings

3/4 c. white wine ☺
6 T. mango chutney
6 T. olive oil
1 T. curry powder

2 lb. boneless chicken breasts,
  skinned
3 T. sesame seeds
Wooden skewers, soaked in water
  for 5 minutes

Mix together wine, chutney, olive oil and curry powder; set aside. Cut chicken breasts into cubes. Pour mixture over chicken and marinate for at least 2 hours. Place chicken on wooden skewers and sprinkle with sesame seeds. Broil or grill for 3 to 5 minutes on each side.

10

 Sesame Chicken Wings

**2 1/2 lb. chicken wings, separated
at joints (discard tips)**

Place chicken wings in a large glass bowl.

MARINADE:

1/2 c. soy sauce	1/3 c. white wine ☺
1/2 tsp. rosemary	1/3 c. red wine ☺
1/2 c. ketchup	1/4 tsp. dry mustard
1 clove garlic, minced	1/2 tsp. Worcestershire sauce
3 thin slices onion	Sesame seeds
2 T. vegetable oil	

Marinade: In blender, combine soy sauce, rosemary, ketchup, garlic, onion, vegetable oil, white wine, red wine, dry mustard and Worcestershire sauce. Blend well. Cover wings with marinade and refrigerate 3 hours, or overnight.

Preheat oven to 350°. Remove chicken wings from marinade. Place on cookie sheet. Brush with marinade. Bake for 45 minutes. Sprinkle with sesame seeds and continue baking another 45 minutes.

"Well behaved women rarely make history!"
--Unknown
(Start misbehavin') BJ

🍷 Wings for a Party

12 servings

Great make-ahead appetizer for any occasion, even a picnic on the beach.

32 chicken wings
3/4 c. white wine ☺
1 T. garlic powder

1 T. Tabasco sauce
1 T. paprika

Cut each chicken wing into three sections, discarding wing tip section. Place white wine, garlic powder, Tabasco and paprika in a heavy plastic bag. Shake bag well to mix. Add chicken. Marinate wings overnight in refrigerator, turning bag several times. Pour entire contents of bag into a large rectangular baking dish. Cover and bake at 375° for 1 hour. Cool. Chill overnight, or freeze drained wings until ready to serve.

To serve: Rewarm in oven or microwave. Serve hot.

🍷 Artichoke Clam Puffs

Makes about 36 pieces

2 pkg. frozen artichoke hearts
1/4 tsp. hot pepper sauce
1 (6 1/2 oz.) can minced clams,
  drained

1 (8 oz.) pkg. cream cheese
3 T. sherry ☺
Paprika

Cook artichokes according to package directions (do not overcook). Drain. Beat cream cheese with pepper sauce and sherry, then stir in clams. Spoon mixture onto cut side of the artichokes and sprinkle with paprika. Broil until browned.

Note: Canned artichoke bottoms may be substituted.

 Salmon Paté

12 servings or 4 lunch servings

4 oz. skinned fresh salmon fillets
1/3 c. dry white wine ☺
1 T. olive oil
3 T. cognac ☺

Freshly-ground pepper
4 oz. best-quality smoked salmon
6 T. safflower or rice oil

Fresh Salmon: Cut fresh salmon into small pieces. In a small pan, combine salmon and wine. Cook over medium-low heat. Remove from heat and drain salmon, discarding wine.

In a small pan, heat olive oil and add salmon. Cook gently over medium heat for about 5 minutes. Do not brown. Add cognac and pepper. Remove from heat and set aside.

Smoked Salmon: Cut smoked salmon into small pieces. In a small saucepan over medium heat, cook smoked salmon in 3 tablespoons oil for 3 to 5 minutes. Cool, then blend fresh salmon and smoked salmon in a food processor with the remaining oil. Refrigerate overnight.

Serve with thin slices of warm toast or sliced French bread.

"Behind every successful woman is herself."
--Unknown

� Chicken liver Pate

18 to 20 servings

1 lb. chicken livers	Zest of 1 lemon, grated
1 med. onion, chopped	2 tsp. salt, divided
3/4 tsp. chopped fresh thyme	1 c. unsalted butter, room temp.
1 bay leaf, crushed	Ground white pepper, to taste
1/2 c. water	2 T. cognac or brandy ☺

Combine livers, onion, thyme, bay leaf, water, lemon zest and 1 teaspoon salt in a 10-inch skillet. Cover and cook for 8 minutes, or until the livers are just cooked through. Do not overcook. Let mixture cool for 10 minutes. Remove liver mixture to food processor work bowl, leaving liquid in the pan. Purée the livers. Add softened butter, 2 tablespoons at a time, blending in well. Scrape down sides of bowl and add 1 teaspoon of salt, white pepper, to taste, and cognac. Blend again for 10 seconds. Pour paté into a 1 1/2-quart mold and chill thoroughly. Serve with French bread, cornichons and spicy Dijon mustard.

Note: May be prepared a day ahead. Recipe is easily halved or doubled.

"Do not start with me. You will NOT win."
--Unknown

Chicken Livers En Brochette

4 servings

1 doz. chicken livers
1 doz. caps from lg. mushrooms
1/4 c. melted butter or margarine

Sherry or Burgundy ☺
Finely-chopped parsley
Salt & pepper

Wash livers and drain dry. Cut in half and thread onto skewers (small ones) alternately with mushroom caps. Brush with the melted butter and sprinkle with the sherry or Burgundy and parsley. Broil until tender, turning several times. This takes only about 15 minutes. As soon as they are heated through, both livers and mushrooms have cooked sufficiently. Sprinkle with salt and coarse pepper and serve.

Sherry Cheese Paté

12 servings

An interesting combination of flavors.

2 (3 oz.) pkg. cream cheese
4 oz. sharp Cheddar cheese,
  grated
2 T. dry sherry ☺

1/2 tsp. curry powder
1/4 tsp. salt
1 (8 oz.) jar chutney
2 green onions & tops

Chop chutney coarsely in blender; reserve. Mix cheese, sherry and seasonings thoroughly. Put on pie plate and chill. Spread chutney over top of cheese and sprinkle with finely-chopped green onions.

15

🍷 Mushroom Flambé

8 to 10 servings

Drink at your own risk. Wine and fire don't work well at my house.

3 T. butter
2 T. oil
1 lb. fresh mushrooms
Salt
Pepper
Tarragon

Chives
Parsley
4 T. sherry ☺
1 T. lemon juice
Few grains sugar
3 T. brandy ☺

Heat butter and oil in chafing dish. Sauté mushrooms. Add herbs, spices, sherry and lemon juice. Cover and cook 3 to 4 minutes. Add sugar and heated brandy and ignite.

Serve on toothpicks.

Note: This recipe is elegant and easy. Make it in your chafing dish.

"Our childhood is what we spend the rest of our lives overcoming."
--Amy Bennett

Liver Paté

1 lb. liverwurst
1/8 tsp. dried thyme leaves
1 T. Worcestershire sauce
1/8 tsp. mace
1 tsp. ground cloves

2 T. sherry ☺
1 T. grated onion
1/4 tsp. pepper
1/4 c. butter or margarine, softened

Peel casing from liverwurst. In medium bowl, mash meat with fork until smooth. Add remaining ingredients, except butter; mix well. Blend in butter until well combined. Pack into serving dish. Cover tightly; refrigerate until ready to use.

Serve with crackers or small slices of rye bread.

Mushroom Chicken Liver Paté

1/4 c. butter
1/2 lb. fresh mushrooms, sliced
1 lb. chicken livers
1 tsp. garlic salt
1 tsp. paprika

1/3 c. finely-chopped green onions
2/3 c. white table wine ☺
3 drops Tabasco
1/2 c. butter
Salt, to taste

Sauté the mushrooms, liver, garlic salt, paprika and onion in butter for 5 minutes. Add wine and Tabasco; cover and cook slowly for 5 to 10 minutes longer. Cool; whirl in blender. Blend in 1/2 cup of softened butter and salt to taste. Turn into dish; chill overnight. Unmold; garnish with parsley and thin lemon slices.

17

Meatball Stroganoff

1/2 c. chopped onion	3 oz. tomato paste
1 T. butter	3 T. bouillon
1/2 lb. sliced mushrooms	2/3 c. sherry ☺
1 lb. lean ground round	1 T. Worcestershire sauce
1 tsp. salt	1 1/2 tsp. celery salt
1/4 tsp. pepper	1/4 c. sliced green pepper
1/2 c. breadcrumbs	1 c. sour cream

Sauté onion in butter; set aside. Sauté mushrooms in butter; set aside. Mix ground round, salt, pepper and breadcrumbs. Form into small meatballs. Sauté meatballs until lightly browned, or place on baking pan in 400° oven for 5 minutes. Combine meatballs, onion, tomato paste, bouillon, sherry, Worcestershire sauce and celery salt. Simmer 20 minutes. Add green pepper and simmer 10 minutes longer. Stir in sour cream and mushrooms and heat just to boiling point. (Do not boil sour cream or it will curdle.)

Note: An inexpensive version of a gourmet recipe which usually uses steak as the meat. It may be prepared a day ahead. Reheat and add sour cream when ready to serve. Keep hot in chafing dish.

"Reality is a hallucination brought on by lack of alcohol."
--Unknown

18

Meatballs with Wine

MEATBALLS:

3 lb. ground beef
2 c. Parmesan cheese, grated
5 eggs
2 tsp. salt
1/8 tsp. pepper

4 cloves garlic, minced
6 slices white bead, soaked &
  squeezed
Enough olive oil to cover bottom
  of pan

SAUCE:

2 1/2 (14 oz.) btl. catsup

2 1/2 c. white wine ☺

Mix meat, cheese, eggs, salt, pepper, garlic and bread. Form meatballs (larger than a marble, but smaller than a golf ball). Brown carefully in olive oil. Make sauce of catsup and wine. Simmer meatballs in sauce 10 minutes in chafing dish.

Make ahead. Refrigerate or freeze. Warm and serve in chafing dish with toothpicks.

"The cardiologist's diet: If it tastes good, spit it out."
--Unknown

Grilled Beef Strips

20 servings

1 lb. round steak, about 1" thick
1 clove garlic, thinly sliced
3 T. sherry ☺
1 tsp. sugar

1/3 c. soy sauce
1 (1") piece fresh ginger, thinly-
   sliced, or 1 tsp. ground ginger

   Remove fat from meat and slice very thin. (It is easier to do if meat is partially frozen.) Mix remaining ingredients and marinate meat strips in mixture for at least 30 minutes. Thread meat on wooden sticks and broil over hot coals.

Swiss Cheese Fondue

8 servings

1 clove garlic
1 1/4 c. Chablis, or any dry white
   wine ☺
1 lb. Swiss cheese, grated

1 T. cornstarch mixed with little
   water
2 T. kirsch ☺

   Rub earthenware fondue pot or ovenproof dish with garlic. Place pot over burner; pour in Chablis and warm it. Add grated cheese. Stir constantly with wooden spoon until cheese melts. Add cornstarch water to cheese, stirring constantly, until thickened. Before serving, add kirsch.

   Note: Serve in chafing dish or fondue dish with French bread cubed, toasted and speared on a fork to dip in fondue.

♛ Beef Tenderloin with Béarnaise Mayonnaise

20 servings

1 (5 to 6 lb.) tenderloin
4 T. dried tarragon
1/3 c. tarragon vinegar
5 shallots, minced
1/2 c. dry white wine ☺
3 lg. egg yolks
2 1/2 T. Dijon mustard

2 T. + 1 tsp. fresh lemon juice
Salt & freshly-ground pepper, to
 taste
1 1/4 c. vegetable oil
1 c. olive oil
1/4 c. tomato paste

Roast tenderloin to desired doneness; chill and slice. Place tarragon, shallots, vinegar and wine in a small saucepan. Heat on medium-high. Reduce liquid to 1 tablespoon; set aside. Place yolks, mustard, lemon juice, salt and pepper in a food processor. Process with a steel blade for 12 seconds, adding oils in a thin steady stream to form a thick emulsion. Add tomato paste and shallot mixture. Process to blend and chill. Serve with beef tenderloin and a variety of rolls.

Very good!

"Maybe it's true that life begins at fifty...but everything else starts to wear out, fall out, or spread out."
--Unknown

Brie, Roquefort and Wild Mushroom Fondue

6 to 8 servings

1 1/2 tsp. olive oil
4 oz. fresh shiitake mushrooms,
  stemmed, caps diced
1 shallot, minced
1 tsp. chopped fresh thyme
1 1/2 T. all-purpose flour
12 oz. chilled 60% (double crème)
  Brie cheese (do not use triple
  crème)

2 oz. chilled Roquefort cheese
1 1/4 c. dry white wine ☺
1 (13 oz.) loaf crusty white bread,
  cut into 1 1/2" cubes
Vegetables (such as carrot sticks,
  blanched broccoli, cauliflower &
  boiled small potatoes)

Heat oil in heavy medium skillet over medium-high heat. Add mushrooms, shallot and thyme; sauté until mushrooms just begin to soften, about 2 minutes. Place flour in a large bowl. Cut rind from Brie; discard rind. Cut Brie into cubes; drop into flour. Toss to coat; separate cheese cubes. Crumble Roquefort into same bowl; toss to coat. Place wine in heavy medium saucepan and bring to simmer over medium heat. Add cheese by handfuls, stirring until melted after each addition. Continue stirring until smooth. Stir mushroom mixture into fondue. Season with a generous amount of pepper. Transfer to fondue pot. Set pot over candle or canned heat burner. Serve with bread and vegetables.

Chicken Fondue in Ginger Broth

6 servings

FONDUE COOKING STOCK:

4 c. chicken stock

3/4 c. white wine ☺

2 lemon slices

2 lg. cloves garlic, minced

2 T. minced ginger root

2 tsp. granulated sugar

CHICKEN AND VEGETABLE TRAY:

1 lb. boneless, skinless chicken breasts

1/2 bunch broccoli

1 sm. yellow summer squash or zucchini

2 c. torn Swiss chard or romaine lettuce

1 sweet red pepper or green pepper

1/4 lb. mushrooms

Hot Chili Sauce (recipe follows)

Garlic Sauce (recipe follows)

Fondue Cooking Stock: In fondue pot, electric skillet or electric wok, combine chicken stock, white wine, lemon slices, garlic, ginger and sugar. Just before serving, heat to simmer in fondue pot.

Chicken and Vegetable Tray: Cut chicken into 3/4-inch pieces; place on serving platter. Cut broccoli, summer squash, Swiss chard and sweet pepper into bite-size pieces. Arrange, along with mushrooms, on a separate platter. Using long fondue forks, spear chicken or vegetables; dip into simmering fondue broth to cook. Cook chicken pieces until no longer pink inside and vegetables until tender-crisp. Serve with Hot Chili Sauce or Garlic Sauce for dipping.

Continued on following page.

Continued from preceding page.

GARLIC SAUCE:

2/3 c. light sour cream or low-fat
   yogurt, or a mixture of both

2 cloves garlic, minced
1/4 c. chopped fresh parsley

In a small bowl, combine sour cream, garlic and parsley. For a variation, substitute chopped fresh basil or coriander to taste for the garlic and reduce the parsley to 1 tablespoon.

HOT CHILI SAUCE:

1/3 c. water
2 T. lemon juice or lime juice
1 T. low-sodium soy sauce

1 tsp. granulated sugar
1/4 tsp. hot pepper flakes

In a small bowl, combine water, lemon or lime juice, soy sauce, sugar and hot pepper flakes.

Veggies & Salads

FAVORITE RECIPES
FROM MY COOKBOOK

Recipe Name	Page Number

Squash and Zucchini Casserole

4 to 6 servings

1 T. butter, or 1 T. olive oil	2 tsp. sugar
2 T. white wine ☺	1 T. oregano
2 lg. onions, chopped	1 tsp. basil
1 green pepper, seeded & chopped	1/2 c. chopped fresh parsley
3 to 4 yellow squash, sliced	1/2 lb. grated cheese, any kind
3 to 4 zucchini, sliced	except American

Preheat oven to 350°. Butter a 2 to 3-quart baking dish. In a large skillet, sauté onion and green pepper for about 15 minutes in butter or olive oil until golden; add wine. Mix in a large mixing bowl the yellow squash, zucchini, sugar, oregano, basil and parsley; add onions and green peppers. Spread in prepared baking dish. Sprinkle top with cheese, cover. Bake for 30 to 35 minutes. Remove cover and cook an additional 10 minutes, or until liquid is absorbed.

Serve garnished with toasted sesame seeds.

"When a man opens the door of his car for his wife,
you can be sure of one thing: either the car is new or the wife is."
--Unknown

Creamed Squash Au Gratin

8 to 10 servings

2 lb. yellow squash, sliced
1/2 c. water
1/2 tsp. salt
1/2 tsp. sugar
1/4 c. butter or margarine, softened
1 1/4 c. cubed sharp Cheddar
  cheese
1/4 c. grated Gruyére cheese

1 c. sour cream
1/2 c. chopped onion
1/4 c. dry white wine, to taste ☺
Salt & freshly-ground pepper
1 c. fresh bread crumbs
4 T. melted butter
Grated fresh imported Parmesan
  cheese

Preheat oven to 350°. Butter a 7 1/2 x 11-inch baking dish. Place squash in a large saucepan. Add water, salt and sugar. Cover and cook for 10 to 12 minutes, or until squash is just tender. Drain very well and return to pan. Add butter and cut into squash with a pastry blender until mixture is chunky. Add Cheddar and Gruyére cheese, sour cream, onion and wine. Season with salt and pepper to taste. Mix well. Pour into prepared baking dish. Stir crumbs and melted butter together and sprinkle over squash. Top generously with Parmesan cheese. Bake 30 to 35 minutes, until done.

Variations:
Add 1/2 cup chopped sweet red pepper.
Substitute 2 pounds zucchini, sliced, for yellow squash. Parboil the zucchini for 7 minutes. Substitute 1/4 cup chopped chives for the onion and add 1/8 teaspoon of paprika to the cheese mixture.

⚯ Bourbon Sweet Potatoes

Serves 8

4 lg. sweet potatoes
4 T. unsalted butter
1/4 c. light brown sugar
2 to 3 T. bourbon ☺

1/4 tsp. vanilla
1 T. cinnamon, or more to taste
Salt & pepper, to taste

Preheat oven to 400°. Cook potatoes for about 1 hour, until tender. When cool, peel potatoes, cut flesh into squares and put in an electric mixer. Add remaining ingredients, and whip until well combined and without lumps. Taste and adjust seasoning.

⚯ Scalloped Mushrooms

Serves 4 to 6

1 lb. fresh mushrooms, cleaned &
  sliced
Salt & pepper, to taste

2 c. soft bread crumbs
1/2 c. melted butter
1/3 c. dry white wine ☺

Place 1/3 of the mushrooms in a buttered casserole. Cover with 1/3 of the bread crumbs and drizzle with 1/3 of the melted butter. Sprinkle salt and pepper. Repeat with another 1/3 of the mushrooms, bread crumbs and butter; sprinkle with salt and pepper. Top with remaining mushrooms, add wine and cover. Bake at 325° for 30 minutes. Combine remaining butter and bread crumbs and spoon over the mushrooms. Bake uncovered for another 10 minutes, until crumbs are lightly browned.

♈ Baked Bell Peppers with Tomatoes

Serves 4 to 6

6 bell peppers (red, yellow &
  green), seeded & cut into strips
  or bite-size pieces
12 oz. cherry tomatoes, stemmed
4 to 5 garlic cloves, coarsely-
  chopped
1/4 c. extra-virgin olive oil
2 T. red wine vinegar, or 2 tsp. each
  balsamic and red wine vinegar ☺

2 tsp. minced fresh oregano,
  marjoram or thyme leaves
1 tsp. sugar, or to taste
Salt & freshly-ground pepper, to
  taste
2 T. fresh basil leaves, torn or
  finely-shredded

Preheat oven to 400°. In a large bowl, mix together the bell peppers, tomatoes, 1/2 of the garlic, the olive oil, 1/2 of the vinegar, the oregano, sugar, salt and pepper. Mix well and spread out in a single layer in a large baking pan.

Roast the vegetables for about 20 minutes. Remove from the oven, turn the vegetables so that they will brown evenly, and return them to the oven. Continue to roast until the peppers are slightly charred at the edges and the tomatoes are soft and tender and have begun to form a sauce, about 10 minutes more.

Remove from the oven and sprinkle with the remaining garlic to taste and the remaining vinegar. Let cool until warm or room temperature. Garnish with the basil just before serving.

🍷 Ham and Sweet Potato Casserole

6 servings

6 med. cooked or canned sweet
  potatoes (yams), cut in halves
3 c. diced or sliced ham
1 glass currant or other tart jelly

3 T. brown sugar
2 T. butter
1/4 c. sherry ☺
Fine buttered crumbs

Combine ham and sweet potatoes in buttered baking dish. Mix jelly, sugar, butter and sherry; pour over ham and sweet potatoes. Top with crumbs and bake at 375° until hot and glazed, about 20 minutes.

🍷 Mustard Mushrooms

4 to 6 servings

8 T. margarine or butter
1 med. onion, chopped
2 med. green peppers, seeded &
  cut into 1" squares
1 lb. fresh mushrooms, cleaned &
  halved

2 T. Dijon mustard
2 T. Worcestershire sauce
1/2 c. brown sugar
3/4 c. mellow red wine ☺
1/2 tsp. salt
Freshly-ground pepper

Melt margarine in a medium saucepan. Sauté chopped onion until soft. Add green peppers and mushrooms, and cook until the mushrooms begin to brown. In a separate bowl, combine mustard, Worcestershire sauce, sugar, wine, salt and pepper together. Mix well. Add mixture to the saucepan. Cook, uncovered, over medium heat until the mixture has reduced and thickened, stirring occasionally. Serve hot.

Note: Great with beef and chicken.

29

Mushrooms in Cognac Herb Sauce

8 to 10 servings

1/2 c. butter	1 tsp. dried thyme
2 lb. sm. mushroom caps	1 tsp. dried basil
4 shallots, minced	1/2 tsp. turmeric
Salt & freshly-ground pepper	1/2 tsp. cumin
1/2 c. cognac, heated ☺	1/2 tsp. coriander
3 cloves garlic	1/2 tsp. ginger
1 T. chopped fresh parsley	1/2 tsp. freshly-ground pepper
1 tsp. dried rosemary	3 c. whipping cream

In a large skillet, sauté shallots and mushroom caps in butter for 2 minutes. Season with salt and pepper. Stir in heated cognac, ignite and stir until flame dies; set aside. In blender or food processor, process garlic, parsley, rosemary, thyme, basil, turmeric, cumin, coriander, ginger, pepper and cream. Add mixture to mushrooms. Put in heavy saucepan and cook over low heat until thick, approximately 3 hours, stirring occasionally.

Serve as a condiment with turkey or beef. It is also wonderful with wild rice.

Note: Fresh herbs may be substituted for dried. Triple the amount.

"Wine...cheerish God and man."
--Judges 9:13

Southwestern Chili Beans

6 or more servings

Almost any kind of beans will be good cooked this way.

1 lb. pink or red beans	**1 1/4 c. Zinfandel or other red**
Cold water	**wine ☺**
1 qt. boiling water	**1 (8 oz.) can tomato sauce**
2 onions, chopped	**2 T. chili powder**
1 clove garlic, chopped	**1/2 tsp. cumin seed**
6 slices bacon, finely cut	**2 tsp. salt**

Wash beans; soak overnight in cold water. Drain. Put in heavy kettle with boiling water and remaining ingredients. Cover; simmer gently until beans are tender and sauce is thick and rich, 3 to 4 hours. Stir often, adding a little more water if needed.

"Boys will be boys, and so will a lot of middle-aged men."
--Kim Hubbard

♉ Sugar Snaps and Mushrooms

4 servings

1/4 c. butter
1/2 sweet onion, sliced &
  separated into rings
1/2 lb. fresh cremini mushrooms,
  cut in half
2 cloves garlic, pressed

1/2 tsp. salt, or to taste
1/2 c. white wine ☺
1/2 c. chicken broth
1 lg. carrot, peeled & julienne-cut
1/2 lb. fresh sugar snap peas

Melt butter in a large saucepan. Add sweet onions, mushrooms, garlic and salt; cook, stirring often, until onions are translucent and mushrooms release their liquid, about 5 minutes. Add white wine and cook 1 minute, stirring to get any browned bits from the bottom of the pan. Then add chicken broth, julienned carrots and sugar snap peas. Cover and simmer an additional 5 minutes, until vegetables are crisp tender.

"Is that a gun in your pocket, or are you just glad to see me?"
--Mae West

♎ Elegant Spinach

6 servings

Very rich, but good!

2 lb. fresh spinach
4 T. butter
1 tsp. lime or lemon juice
1 tsp. Worcestershire sauce

1/2 c. sour cream
1/4 lb. fresh mushrooms, sliced
5 T. dry sherry ☺
Salt & pepper, to taste

Wash spinach thoroughly in cold water several times. Place in a saucepan with only the water that is remaining on the leaves. Cover and cook over medium heat for about 10 minutes, until just tender. Drain well and chop fine. Combine 2 tablespoons butter, lime juice, Worcestershire sauce and sour cream in a large skillet. Stir in spinach. Sauté mushrooms in remaining butter. Add sherry, seasonings and mushrooms to spinach. Mix and simmer for 2 to 3 minutes. Serve at once.

"Men are like steel. When they lose their temper, they lose their worth."
--Chuck Norris

Green Beans with Mint

8 to 10 servings

1 T. salt, plus more, to taste
3 lb. green beans, ends trimmed
1 1/3 c. white wine ☺
1 lg. white onion, peeled & cut
  crosswise into 1/8" thick slices
3 T. sugar
1 shallot, minced

2 tsp. Dijon mustard
1 T. chopped fresh mint (this is a
  key ingredient)
2 T. white wine vinegar
5 T. olive oil
Freshly-ground pepper, to taste

Bring a large saucepan 2/3 full of water to a boil over high heat. Add the 1 tablespoon salt and the green beans, and cook until the beans are bright green and tender, 4 to 5 minutes. Drain and immerse the beans in a bowl of ice water to cool, then drain and set aside.

In a small saucepan, over medium heat, combine the white wine, onion, sugar and salt to taste. Bring to a boil, separating the onion slices into rings, and cook until slightly tender, 1 to 2 minutes. Remove from the heat and let cool.

In a small bowl, whisk together the shallot, mustard, mint and vinegar. Gradually whisk in 4 tablespoons of the olive oil. Season with salt and pepper and set the vinaigrette aside.

In a large sauté pan, over medium heat, warm the remaining 1 tablespoon olive oil and add the beans. Sauté, stirring occasionally, until they are warmed through, 2 to 3 minutes. Drain the onions, discarding the vinaigrette mixture, and add the onions to the beans. Cook until warmed through, about 2 minutes more. Add the vinaigrette and toss well to coat. Transfer to a warmed serving dish.

Wild Rice Forestiere

8 to 10 servings

1 c. wild rice
1 c. mild white Cheddar cheese,
  shredded, divided
3/4 c. sliced mushrooms, sautéed
1/2 c. chopped onion
1/2 c. hot water
1/2 c. vegetable oil

2 (16 oz.) cans tomatoes, drained,
  reserving juices & chopped
1 tsp. salt
1/4 tsp. freshly-ground pepper
1/2 tsp. basil
1/3 c. sherry ☺

Rinse rice and soak in water for at least 24 hours, preferably 48 hours. Drain rice.

Preheat oven to 350°. In a large bowl, combine 1/2 cup cheese, mushrooms, onion, hot water, oil, chopped tomatoes, 1 cup reserved juice, salt, pepper, basil and sherry. Pour into 2-quart baking dish. Cover and bake for 1 hour and 45 minutes. During the last 5 minutes, sprinkle remaining cheese on top of casserole to melt.

"If you can't convince them, confuse them."
--Harry Truman

 Carrots Cointreau

6 servings

Very good!

30 fresh baby carrots	**1/4 c. honey**
2 T. cointreau ☺	**1 1/2 T. fresh lemon juice**
1/4 c. brandy ☺	**2 T. fresh parsley, chopped**

Parboil peeled baby carrots in boiling salted water for 5 minutes. Drain. Place carrots into buttered 1 1/2-quart baking dish. In a small bowl, combine cointreau, brandy, honey and lemon juice. Pour mixture over the carrots. Toss to coat carrots. Bake at 350° for 15 minutes. Stir, Sprinkle with parsley and serve.

 Carrots with White Grapes

2 servings

Brainless to fix and good.

1 (13 1/2 oz.) jar sm. whole	**4 T. butter**
Belgium carrots	**3 T. cointreau** ☺
20 seedless white grapes	

Drain carrots. In a skillet, melt butter; add cointreau, stir. Add grapes and carrots and heat through.

36

 Squash Risotto

4 servings

Good, but stay focused. Drink wine at your own risk.

2 c. acorn squash 'balls' (use melon
  baller)
2 oz. extra-virgin olive oil
1/2 c. chopped onion
2 cloves minced garlic
2/3 c. good white wine ☺

2 to 3 c. rich chicken broth
1 T. minced rosemary (I use fresh)
1/2 c. freshly-grated Parmesan
  cheese
1/2 c. toasted sunflower seeds
Salt & pepper

Heat a thick bottomed pot large enough to accommodate almost all of the squash in a single layer. Heat the pot until it is very hot, then in quick succession, add the oil and squash. Stir the squash quickly as it caramelizes and the outside of the balls begin to darken. When they are well toasted, reduce the heat to medium and add the onions. Stir for a few minutes as the onion also caramelizes a bit. Add the garlic, and stir a minute more. Add the white wine and stir as is reduces, coating the squash. Reduce the heat to low. Add 1/2 of the chicken broth and rosemary, and continue stirring as the squash cooks. If needed, add more of the chicken broth until the squash is just cooked. Adjust the heat as needed, trying to evaporate the liquid and glaze, and cook the squash simultaneously. When the squash is tender (not mushy), add the cheese, sunflower seeds and season to taste with the salt and pepper.

Rice with Spinach and Feta Cheese

6 servings

3 T. olive oil
1 lg. onion, finely-chopped
2 lg. garlic cloves, minced
1 1/4 c. uncooked long-grain rice
2 c. chicken broth
1/3 c. dry white wine ☺
1 1/2 (10 oz.) pkg. fresh baby
 spinach leaves (remove any large
 stems), very coarsely-chopped

2 med. tomatoes, seeded &
 chopped
1 c. crumbled Feta cheese (or bleu
 cheese)
Salt & freshly-ground black
 pepper, to taste

In large heavy saucepan, heat the oil over medium heat. Add the onions and garlic; and cook, stirring, about 5 minutes, or until soft. Add the rice and stir about 2 minutes, or until the rice is translucent. Carefully add the chicken broth and wine. Stir to mix well and bring to a boil. Reduce the heat to low, cover and cook about 15 minutes, or until the rice is almost tender. Stir in the spinach; cover and cook another 8 minutes, or until all the liquid has been absorbed. Mix in the tomatoes and cheese, and season with salt and pepper. Serve immediately.

German Red Cabbage

8 to 10 servings

1/2 lb. bacon, diced
1 head red cabbage, cored &
 thinly-sliced
2 tsp. salt
2 to 3 c. dry red wine ☺

1 to 2 c. water
1/2 c. sugar
6 T. white vinegar
3 tart apples, peeled, cored &
 sliced

Brown bacon in a large Dutch oven. Add cabbage and stir over medium heat until cabbage starts to glisten and wilt. Add salt, wine and water. Bring to boil; cover, reduce heat and simmer for 1 hour. Add sugar, vinegar and apples; cover and simmer for another hour. If mixture becomes too dry, mix 2 parts red wine to 1 part water and add as needed.

Great with beef or pork.

"A table without wine is like a stew without meat."
--Spanish Proverb

Almond Wild Rice

8 to 10 servings

1/2 c. golden raisins*	1 c. brown rice
1/4 c. dry sherry ☺	1 c. slivered almonds
1 c. wild rice	1/2 c. chopped fresh parsley
4 c. chicken broth, boiling	Salt & freshly-ground pepper, to
6 T. butter	taste

Bring raisins and sherry to a boil in a small saucepan. Reduce heat and simmer for 5 minutes; set aside. Combine wild rice, 2 cups boiling stock and 2 tablespoons butter in a double boiler over simmering water; cook, covered, for 1 1/4 hours. Place brown rice, remaining boiling stock and 2 tablespoons butter in a heavy medium saucepan. Bring to boil, reduce heat to low and cook until all water is absorbed, about 40 minutes.

Meanwhile, sauté almonds in the remaining 2 tablespoons butter in a small skillet over low heat until lightly toasted. Combine wild rice, brown rice, raisins with sherry, almonds and parsley in a large mixing bowl. Season to taste with salt and pepper, stirring to combine. Transfer to a serving bowl and serve immediately.

*You can soak the raisins in orange juice or sherry overnight, and they will be really plump and taste great.

"Whether you think you can, or that you can't, you are usually right."
--Henry Ford

♟ Molded Melon Ball Salad

10 to 12 servings

The contrast in color is beautiful.

2 T. (env.) plain or lemon gelatin	**1 c. sweet white wine ☺**
1 1/2 c. pineapple juice	**4 c. sm. melon balls (honeydew,**
1 c. melon juices (drain melon	**cantaloupe & watermelon)**
balls well)	**1/2 c. blueberries, for garnish**

Soften gelatin in 1/2 cup cold pineapple juice for 5 minutes. Dissolve in remaining boiling pineapple juice. Add melon juice. Chill until partially thickened, stirring the mixture over ice cubes to hasten the chilling. Pour a thin layer of the thickened gelatin mixture into a 2-quart ring mold. Arrange a few melon balls to make a design in the gelatin; chill until firm. Mix remaining balls with gelatin and fill mold; chill until firm.

To serve: Unmold on salad greens. Serve with whipped cream and mayonnaise, equal parts. Scatter fresh blueberries among the melon balls.

"The problem with some people is that when they aren't drunk they're sober."
--William Butler Yeats

Party Cherry Mold

8 servings

When fresh sweet cherries are in season, substitute them for the canned fruit.

2 pkg. cherry-flavored gelatin dessert
2 c. boiling water & cherry juice
1 c. port ☺

1 (No. 2 1/2) can black sweet cherries, pitted, well drained
1 (3 oz.) pkg. cream cheese
Pecan halves

Dissolve gelatin in boiling water and cherry juice and cool. Add port. Chill until mixture begins to thicken. Spoon a little of the mixture into the bottom of your mold. Arrange in it cherries stuffed with cream cheese and pecans. Roll cream cheese into little balls to stuff the cherries, and top each ball with a pecan. Arrange nut-side down in the mold. Chill until firm. Then carefully spoon in the rest of the thickened gelatin, adding the other cherries which needn't be stuffed. Chill until firm.

Note: It may take you several glasses of wine to stuff all the cherries, but worth it. Time consuming.

"Most women put off entertaining until the kids are grown."
--Erma Bombeck

Potato Salad with White Wine

4 or more servings

There's remarkable flavor here for such a simple mixture.

8 sm. new potatoes, cooked in jackets
1/2 c. white wine ☺
1/2 bunch young onions, with tops, sliced

1/4 c. salad oil
3 T. tarragon vinegar
1 T. sugar
Salt & pepper
3 T. minced parsley

Peel and slice potatoes while warm, moisten with the wine and add other ingredients. Mix lightly and chill several hours.

"Love may be blind, but marriage is a real eye-opener!"
--Unknown

♀ Shrimp Salad with Wine, in Tomatoes

4 servings

A wine marinade subtly influences the flavor.

1 1/2 c. cooked cleaned shrimp, cut
   in pieces
1/2 c. Sauterne, Chablis or sherry☺
1 c. chopped celery
1/2 c. diced cucumber
3 hard-cooked eggs, chopped
1 tsp. salt

Little pepper
1 c. salad dressing
4 lg. tomatoes, hollowed &
   drained
Crisp salad greens
Walnuts, pecans or pine nuts (opt.)

Add Sauterne to shrimp and chill. Add remaining ingredients, except tomatoes and greens; mix well. Serve in tomato cups on a bed of salad greens.
Note: Another nice presentation.

*"I never drink water because of the disgusting things that fish do in it.
Drink wine."*
                  --W.C. Fields

Avocado, Bacon and Chicken Salad

2 servings

DRESSING:
1 T. peanut oil

1 T. white wine ☺
1/4 tsp. fresh lemon juice

SALAD:
Romaine lettuce
2 chicken breast halves, poached
 & cubed
1 avocado, seeded, peeled & sliced

2 bacon strips, crisp cooked
Crumbled Bleu cheese, or cheese
 of choice
1 tomato, peeled & seeded

Dressing: In a small bowl, whisk peanut oil, white wine and lemon juice.
Salad: Arrange romaine lettuce on 2 plates. Divide remaining ingredients and compose salad on lettuce. Drizzle dressing over each salad.
 I've doubled and tripled this recipe.

*"Creativity is allowing yourself to make mistakes.
Art is knowing which ones to keep."*
--Scott Adams

Grilled Breast of Chicken Salad

4 to 6 servings

MARINADE:
1 c. dry white wine☺
5 T. Dijon mustard

3 to 4 whole chicken breasts,
  skinned & halved

DRESSING:
1 c. mayonnaise
2 T. A-1 sauce
1 T. Dijon mustard

1/2 tsp. dill weed
Half & half
Salt & freshly-ground pepper

SALAD:
Chopped lettuce
Green bell pepper strips

Red bell pepper strips
Onions

Marinade: Blend white wine and mustard. Marinate the boneless, skinless chicken breasts for at least an hour.

Dressing: Combine mayonnaise, A-1 sauce, Dijon mustard and dill weed. Blend and thin with half & half, as necessary.

Salad: Cook onions and peppers over medium heat in a small amount of oil until very tender, about 10 minutes. Keep warm. Grill chicken breasts about 5 minutes on each side. Sprinkle with salt and pepper.

Place bed of lettuce on individual plates and top with a few tablespoons of dressing. Slice grilled chicken breasts horizontally and place on top of lettuce. Spoon more dressing on top of the chicken. Top this with sautéed onions and peppers that are still warm from the frying pan.

Seafood Mousse Louise

10 to 12 servings

2 T. (env.) unflavored gelatin
1/3 c. sherry ☺
1/2 c. boiling water
1 1/4 c. mayonnaise
1 c. chili sauce
1 T. lemon juice
1/2 c. heavy cream, whipped
1 c. flaked cooked or canned
  crabmeat
1 c. finely-cut (with scissors)
  cooked or canned shrimp

6 hard-cooked eggs, grated
1 (4 oz.) can chopped ripe olives,
  drained (opt.)
2 T. chopped parsley
2 T. pimiento
1 tsp. grated onion
1 tsp. grated lemon peel
1 tsp. Worcestershire sauce
Dash of Tabasco sauce
Dash of salt & pepper

   Soften gelatin in sherry for 5 minutes, dissolve in boiling water; cool. Blend mayonnaise, chili sauce and lemon juice. Add gelatin; fold in whipped cream. Add all remaining ingredients; mix lightly but thoroughly. Turn into 2 (1-quart) molds, or 10 to 12 individual molds, rinsed with cold water. Chill until firm.

   Unmold on crisp greens and garnish as you wish, possibly with slices of tomato and avocado, ripe olives and celery curls.

Avocado - Lime Mousse

6 servings

1 pkg. lime-flavored gelatin
1/2 c. hot water
1/2 c. muscatel or white port
  wine ☺
1/4 c. mayonnaise
1/2 c. heavy cream, whipped
1 T. lime juice

1/2 tsp. onion juice
1/2 tsp. salt
1 c. finely-diced avocado
1/2 c. finely-diced celery
1 T. grated green pepper
Greens
Orange or grapefruit sections

  Dissolve gelatin in hot water and muscatel or port wine (don't boil wine). Chill until slightly thickened. Beat until frothy; blend in mayonnaise, whipped cream, lime juice, onion juice and salt. Fold in avocado, celery and green pepper. Chill in oiled 1-quart ring mold until firm. Unmold on greens, garnish with citrus fruit sections and serve with French dressing.
  Very good.

Deviled Eggs

12 servings

6 hard-boiled eggs (shelled & cut
  in half lengthwise)
Low-fat mayonnaise

Mustard
A touch of sherry ☺

  Remove yolks and mix with mayonnaise, mustard and sherry. Whip and add more mayonnaise or mustard to taste.

48

Hot Potato Salad with Wine

4 to 6 servings

4 to 6 med.-sized potatoes
4 slices bacon
2 T. flour
2/3 to 3/4 c. white wine☺
1/4 c. water
1 T. instant onion, or 1/4 c.
  chopped fresh onion

1 tsp. prepared mustard
1 T. wine vinegar
Salt & pepper, to taste
3 hard-cooked eggs
3/4 c. thinly-sliced celery

Cook potatoes in boiling salted water until tender. Drain, peel and dice them into a heated bowl. Meanwhile, cook bacon until crisp, remove from pan and drain off all but 2 tablespoons fat. Blend in flour. Add wine, water, onion, mustard and vinegar, as well as salt and pepper to taste. Cook and stir until mixture has boiled and thickened. Dice eggs and add to potatoes with celery. Pour hot dressing over salad and mix lightly. Add crumbled bacon and extra salt, if needed.

Serve while warm, or keep warm for serving over hot water.

"I have never hated a man enough to give him his diamonds back."
--Zsa Zsa Gabor

Steak and Spinach Salad with Hot Pan Dressing

Serves 4 to 6

1 1/2 lb. top sirloin
1/2 tsp. salt
1/2 tsp. freshly-ground pepper
1 tsp. butter, divided
1 tsp. olive oil, divided
2 med. Portobello mushroom caps, sliced
2 tsp. minced garlic
1/2 c. red wine

1/2 c. beef broth
1/4 c. balsamic vinegar
1 (6 oz.) pkg. baby spinach, or mixed greens
2 plum tomatoes, sliced
1 sm. red onion
1/2 lemon
1/3 c. crumbled Roquefort cheese or Gorgonzola

Sprinkle steak evenly with salt and pepper. Heat a large nonstick skillet over medium heat for 2 minutes. Melt 1/2 teaspoon butter with 1/2 teaspoon oil. Add steak, and cook until well browned on one side, about 6 minutes. Turn steak and cook 3 more minutes (rare), 4 minutes (medium-rare), or 5 minutes (medium). Remove steak from pan and set aside.

Melt remaining 1/2 teaspoon butter with 1/2 teaspoon oil in skillet over medium heat. Sauté mushrooms and garlic 4 minutes. Stir in wine, broth and balsamic vinegar, stirring to loosen particles from bottoms of skillet. Bring to a boil, reduce heat and cook 4 to 5 minutes.

Toss together spinach, tomatoes, onion and hot mixture in pan; divide evenly between 4 plates. Squeeze lemon, drizzling juice evenly over top. Cut steak into 1/2-inch slices, and arrange over salads. (You may want to sub this part out, depending upon how much wine you've had). Sprinkle cheese evenly over top.

Seafood

FAVORITE RECIPES
FROM MY COOKBOOK

Recipe Name	Page Number

Brazilian Stuffed Whitefish

6 servings

3 lb. whitefish or trout	1 bay leaf
2 T. butter	3/4 lb. cooked shrimp
1 onion, chopped	3/4 c. bread crumbs
1 tsp. salt	1 c. white table wine ☺
1/4 tsp. pepper	1 pt. oysters (opt.)
1 T. minced parsley	

Have your fish dealer clean and scale the fish, leaving head and tail intact. Wash in cold water and dry. For stuffing, melt butter in a skillet; add onion, salt, pepper, parsley and bay leaf. Cook until onion is lightly browned. Sauté shrimp a minute in the same skillet, then add crumbs and liquid from oysters. Stuff fish rather loosely and close cavity by inserting skewers at intervals and lacing with string. Place in shallow baking pan with wine. Brush well with butter and bake at 400° for 45 minutes, basting with the wine occasionally, if you like. Add oysters to pan last 5 minutes. They are a garnish.

"In my house I'm the boss, my wife is just the decision maker."
--Woody Allen
(And don't ever forget it!)

Tilapia with Lime Caper Sauce

6 servings

1/4 tsp. garlic powder	Sweet Hungarian paprika
1/2 tsp. onion powder	1 T. olive oil
1/2 tsp. dill weed	2 T. butter, divided use
1 tsp. lemon pepper	1 c. white wine ☺
1/4 c. grated Parmesan cheese	Juice of half a lime
2 tsp. mayonnaise	2 T. sm. capers
6 boneless tilapia fillets, catfish,	Chopped parsley & lime slices, for
trout or snapper	garnish
Salt, to taste	

Combine garlic powder, onion powder, dill weed, lemon pepper and Parmesan cheese. Using half of the mayonnaise, brush one side of each tilapia fillet. Sprinkle with half of the spice mixture, then sprinkle lightly with paprika. Turn fillets over and repeat using the remainder of the mayonnaise and spice mixture.

Heat a large, heavy skillet over medium heat until very hot, but not smoking. Add the olive oil and 1 tablespoon of the butter. Swirl to coat the bottom of the pan. Quickly fry tilapia on both sides until golden, turning only once. Remove fish to a platter and keep warm.

Carefully pour the wine into the hot pan. Boil for 1 minute, stirring to scrape up any browned bits from the bottom of the pan. Add lime juice and continue cooking over medium heat until sauce becomes syrupy and reduced to about 1/4 cup. Whisk in remaining 1 tablespoon of butter and capers. Spoon sauce over warm tilapia and garnish with chopped parsley and lime slices.

♀ Teriyaki Swordfish

6 to 8 servings

4 swordfish steaks, 1 1/4" to 1 1/2"
  thick

MARINADE:

1 1/3 c. light soy sauce	**4 tsp. freshly-grated ginger root**
2/3 c. sherry ☺	**2 cloves garlic, crushed**
2 tsp. sugar	

Place swordfish in 1 or 2 low flat dishes that will hold them in one layer. In a small saucepan, bring soy sauce, sherry, sugar, ginger root and garlic to a boil over medium heat. Strain marinade over steaks. Cover lightly and refrigerate for at least 2 hours.

Heat gas or charcoal grill. Grill steaks 5 to 6 minutes per side. Baste with marinade several times while grilling. Serve immediately.

Variation: Try salmon steaks.

"Wine gives courage and makes men more apt for passion."
--Ovid

♱ Spicy Swordfish with Tomato and Orange Sauce

4 servings

1/2 c. olive oil
1 sm. red onion, finely chopped
3 garlic cloves, minced
1 T. minced fresh basil, or 1 tsp. dried
2 tsp. red pepper flakes
2/3 c. dry white wine or dry vermouth ☺
1/2 c. orange juice, plus 1 orange, peeled & cut into sections

3 T. fresh lime juice
3 med. tomatoes, coarsely chopped
2 T. chopped parsley
1/2 tsp. salt
1/4 tsp. black pepper
4 swordfish steaks, 1/2" to 3/4" thick
3 scallions, chopped

Preheat the broiler. In a large skillet, warm 1/4 cup of the oil over medium heat. Add the onion, garlic, basil and red pepper flakes; cook, stirring until the onion is softened but not browned, about 5 minutes. Add the wine, orange juice and lemon juice; increase the heat to high and cook until reduced to a syrup, 4 to 6 minutes. Add the tomatoes and cook just until heated through, about 1 minute. Stir in the parsley, salt and pepper; cover and remove from heat.

Arrange the swordfish on a broiler pan and brush each with 1 tablespoon of the oil. Broil the swordfish 2 to 3 inches from the heat for about 5 minutes per side (depending on the thickness), until almost opaque.

Spoon some sauce onto a broiler-proof serving platter and arrange the fish on top. Spoon more sauce over the fish and top with the orange sections and scallions. Set the platter under the broiler to heat the oranges and allow the fish to finish cooking, about 2 minutes. Serve hot.

Shrimp - Stuffed Trout

6 to 8 servings

6 whole trout, boned
Flour
2 eggs, beaten
2 c. bread crumbs

1/4 c. butter
Juice & grated zest of 1 lemon
Salt & pepper

SHRIMP STUFFING:
1 lg. onion, chopped
3 c. sliced mushrooms
2 T. butter
1 tsp. salt
1 1/4 tsp. white pepper

1/4 c. diced sweet red pepper
1/4 c. diced green onions
1/2 lb. bay shrimp, cooked
2 1/4 c. dry sherry ☺

Shrimp Stuffing: Sauté onion and mushrooms in butter in skillet until lightly browned. Add salt, white pepper, red pepper, green onions, shrimp and sherry. Simmer over medium heat until liquid is reduced to glaze, stirring occasionally. Cool.

Make trout: Dredge each trout in flour, dip in eggs, then roll in bread crumbs to coat lightly. Carefully fill each trout cavity with shrimp stuffing. Secure seams with wood picks. Melt butter in large skillet. Sauté trout in butter, a few at a time, until lightly browned on both sides and stuffing is hot. Remove trout when done and keep warm.

Add lemon juice and zest to butter remaining in pan and heat few seconds. Season to taste with salt and pepper. Pour over trout.

Trout Marquery

2 servings

2 (6 to 8 oz.) tenderloins of trout
1/2 c. white wine ☺
1 bay leaf
1/2 lb. shrimp, boiled & chopped
2 c. Hollandaise sauce

1 T. olive oil
2 c. water
5 peppercorns
1 tsp. lemon juice
1/2 c. fresh mushrooms, sliced

Mix the oil, water, wine, peppercorns, bay leaf and lemon juice, and poach trout in the mixture for 10 to 15 minutes. Add the chopped shrimp and mushrooms to the Hollandaise and pour over the cooked trout.

"I never forget a face, but in your case I'll be glad to make an exception."
--Groucho Marx

Grilled Salmon with Mustard Dill Sauce

4 servings

MUSTARD DILL SAUCE:

4 T. dark, spicy prepared mustard
1 tsp. dry mustard
3 T. sugar or honey
2 T. white wine ☺

1/3 c. vegetable oil
3 T. fresh chopped dill, or 1 1/2 tsp. dried dill

4 salmon, swordfish or haddock steaks

Extra-virgin olive oil

Mustard Dill Sauce: In a small bowl, mix mustards, sugar and vinegar to a paste. Slowly whisk in oil until sauce is consistency of mayonnaise. Stir in dill. Store in refrigerator and serve with fish or grilled chicken.
Makes 2/3 cup sauce.

Fish: Rinse salmon under cold water, drain and pat dry with paper towels. Sprinkle steaks with olive oil.

Heat barbecue grill, grill pan, cast-iron skillet or a nonstick skillet until very hot. Place steaks in pan and grill for about 4 to 5 minutes per side. They should be browned and just done. Transfer to serving platter and serve immediately with mustard dill sauce.

"Drink is the feast of reason and the flow of soul."
--Faulkner

♉ Seared Salmon with Orange Glaze

6 servings

6 (6 oz.) salmon fillets, skinned if desired
1 T. sesame oil, preferably untoasted
3 tsp. low-sodium soy sauce
1/3 c. white wine ☺

1 c. fresh-squeezed orange juice
1 tsp. dry or minced orange zest
3 T. sherry ☺
1/2 tsp. peeled, grated or minced ginger root
2 thin slices orange, unpeeled

Pat salmon dry. Preheat oven to 400°. Have a glass baking dish ready, large enough to hold salmon in a single layer.

In a large skillet over medium-high heat, heat oil. Add salmon and sear, turning once, 1 minute on each side. You should hear fish sizzle. Transfer salmon to baking dish and drizzle with soy sauce and wine. Transfer to oven and roast 10 minutes, until cooked through and flakes easily.

Meanwhile, in a small saucepan over medium-high heat, heat orange juice and zest, sherry and ginger. Simmer, stirring frequently, about 15 minutes until sauce is reduced by half and thickened. Add orange slices and cook, stirring once or twice. Remove from heat. Transfer salmon to individual plates. Drizzle with sauce and serve immediately.

"Love is temporary insanity curable by marriage."
--Ambrose Bierce

⚦ Herb-Crusted Salmon with Sun-Dried Tomato Sauce

4 servings

This is a great dish!

4 tsp. olive oil
2 T. shallots, minced
1 T. lemon juice, strained
1/2 c. dry white wine ☺
6 sun-dried tomatoes (not packed
 in oil), finely minced
1/2 tsp. coarse salt
1/2 tsp. fresh ground black pepper

1 T. fresh basil, minced, or 1 tsp.
 crumbled dried basil
1 T. fresh thyme, minced, or 1 tsp.
 crumbled dried thyme
2 tsp. fresh rosemary leaves,
 minced, or 1/2 tsp. crumbled
 dried rosemary
1/2 c. dry bread crumbs
2 (12 oz.) skinless salmon fillets

In a 10-inch nonstick skillet, heat 2 teaspoons of oil over medium heat. Add shallots and sauté, stirring constantly, until lightly golden, about 1 minute. Add lemon juice, wine and sun-dried tomatoes. Turn heat to medium-high and cook until sauce is reduced to 1/2 cup, about 2 minutes. Season with salt and pepper and set aside. (Sauce can be made up to 1 hour before cooking fish. Reheat over low heat just before removing fish from oven.)

Adjust oven rack to center of oven and preheat to 400°. Lightly grease a 9x13x2-inch ovenproof casserole with cooking spray, set aside.

On a flat plate, combine basil, thyme, rosemary and bread crumbs. Dredge each fillet in bread crumb mixture, coating well. Transfer fillets to prepared pan and place 2 inches apart. Drizzle with remaining 2 teaspoons of oil. Bake in a preheated oven just until fish is opaque and barely flakes when tested in the center with a knife, about 8 to 10 minutes. Transfer to serving platter, slice each fillet in half crosswise, spoon sauce over fillets and serve.

59

Easy Herbed Grilled Salmon

4 servings

You can grill the salmon or bake in oven at 350° until done.

Vegetable oil spray
1 lb. boneless salmon filet, about
  1" thick (large end preferred)
1 lime
3 T. white wine ☺
2 tsp. mayonnaise or butter
1 tsp. kosher salt

1 tsp. onion powder
1 tsp. garlic powder
1 tsp. lemon pepper
1 tsp. dried oregano
1 tsp. dried basil
1 tsp. dried dill weed
1/2 tsp. sweet paprika

Preheat grill to high heat. Make a tray out of a doubled length of heavy-duty foil large enough for the salmon filet, by folding a large piece in half and folding up all four sides, with the dull-side up. (The shiny side reflects, so you want it down so as not to burn the food). Spray the entire inside of the foil tray liberally with cooking spray. Place the foil tray on a platter or metal tray to transport to the grill. Place the salmon filet in the foil tray, skin-side down (or boned-side up if it is skinned). Squeeze lime juice over salmon and sprinkle with white wine. Spread top of salmon with the mayonnaise or butter.

In a small bowl, mix together kosher salt, onion powder, garlic powder, lemon pepper, oregano, basil and dill weed. Sprinkle the mixture evenly over the top of the salmon, then top with the sweet paprika.

Place baking pan with foil tray on hot grill. Transfer the foil tray to the hot grill. Cook in a hot covered grill for 10 minutes per inch of thickness of the fish filet. Do not overcook or it will be dry and unpalatable. Turning is not necessary. Salmon is done when it turns a light pink color throughout and feels firm when pressed gently with the back of a fork. Whitefish is done when it turns opaque. This method works best with large, thick fillets. Use a spatula to lift the salmon away from the skin to serve. Garnish with lime slices.

Broiled Pompano

4 servings

1 to 2 pompano, or turbot, or
  Dover sole, or 4 filets, split &
  boned
Salt & pepper
1/2 c. butter, melted

1/2 c. dry vermouth ☺
Fine, dry bread crumbs
Grated Cheddar cheese, or
  Parmesan cheese

    Season fish with salt and pepper; broil until brown on each side, basting twice with the butter and wine. When almost done, sprinkle with crumbs and cheese and give the fish a minute more. Total cooking time shouldn't exceed 8 minutes.

"If at first you don't succeed, try, try again. Then give up.
There's no use in being a damn fool about it."
--W.C. Fields

Filet of Sole

3 to 4 servings

6 filets of sole	**8 mushroom caps**
2 T. lemon juice	**2 T. butter**
1/2 c. Chablis ☺	**3 T. flour**
1/4 c. water	**2 T. tarragon vinegar**
1/2 tsp. salt	**3/4 c. liquid from sole**
1/8 tsp. freshly-ground pepper	**1/2 c. cream**
1 bay leaf	**2 egg yolks, beaten**

Arrange filets in baking dish and pour the lemon juice, wine and water over them. Add salt, pepper and bay leaf. Cover the dish with aluminum foil and bake at 350° for 15 minutes. Transfer sole to a hot serving dish. Sauté mushroom caps in butter. Remove from pan. Add to the butter the flour and vinegar, stirring until smooth. Add liquid from sole, cream and egg yolks and cook, stirring constantly until sauce is thickened. Do not overcook. Remove from heat. Pour over sole and serve immediately, garnished with mushroom caps.

"Eat thy bread with joy, and drink thy wine with a merry heart."
--Ecclesiastes 9:10

Tuna Steaks in Marinade

4 to 6 servings

4 (1" thick) fresh red tuna steaks

MARINADE:
1/4 c. vegetable oil
1 tsp. hot chili sesame oil
1/4 c. rice wine vinegar
1 T. packed brown sugar

3 T. Madeira wine or sweet
  vermouth ☺
1/4 c. soy sauce
1/4 tsp. ground ginger
1/4 tsp. minced garlic

Place tuna steaks in shallow glass dish, large enough to hold steaks in one layer.

Marinade: Whisk oil, sesame oil, rice wine vinegar, brown sugar, Madeira wine, soy sauce, ginger and garlic in a small bowl. Pour over tuna steaks. Cover and let marinate in refrigerator at least 3 hours, turning occasionally.

Grill over charcoal or gas grill until just cooked through, 5 to 6 minutes per side. Do not overcook. Baste with marinade while cooking to keep moist.

"I suppose we all have our recollections of our earlier holidays,
all bristling with horror."
--Flann O'Brien

Peppered Ahi Tuna with Mushrooms and Port Wine

4 servings

4 (6 oz.) portions Ahi tuna
3 T. crushed black peppercorns
1 T. canola oil
1 lb. mushrooms, sliced
2 oz. leeks, sliced
2 tsp. chopped garlic
2 tsp. chopped shallots

2 c. port wine ☺
2 T. sweet butter
2 lg. russet potatoes, peeled
3 oz. sweet butter
4 to 6 oz. milk
Salt & pepper, to taste

First, prepare mushrooms by heating clarified butter in a medium sauté pan. Add leeks and sauté until done. Add mushrooms, shallots and garlic; sauté until tender. Deglaze the pan with port wine and finish with 2 tablespoons butter. Season with salt and pepper to taste.

Prepare potatoes. Place potatoes in cold water to cover and bring to a boil. Cook until tender, strain and push through a ricer or food mill. Stir in hot milk and butter and season to taste with salt and pepper.

Finally, cook tuna and assemble the dish. To cook the fish, heat a nonstick pan over high heat. Add 1 tablespoon oil. Lightly coat tuna with crushed peppercorns. Sear Ahi tuna until rare (about 1 1/2 minutes on each side, I cook mine longer, personal preference). Serve with rice or mashed potatoes and top with port wine/mushroom mixture.

♀ Fresh Clams with Artichokes and Tomatoes

4 servings

4 med. to lg. artichokes
1 lemon
1/4 c. olive oil
3/4 c. fresh bread crumbs
1 sm. onion, finely diced
3 lg. garlic cloves, minced
3 med. tomatoes, peeled, seeded & chopped
1 sprig fresh thyme, or a pinch of dried
1 c. homemade fish stock, light chicken stock, or reduced-sodium canned chicken broth

1/2 c. dry white wine or dry vermouth ☺
1/4 to 1/2 tsp. crushed hot red pepper, to taste
2 doz. sm. clams, well scrubbed
2 T. minced fresh basil
Salt & freshly-ground black pepper
1 lb. hot cooked linguine or spaghetti

With a small sharp knife, cut away the top of each artichoke. Cut a flat bottom on each, then peel away all the leaves from the bottoms. Remove the fuzzy choke and trim the bottoms down to a neat white portion. Cut the lemon in half and squeeze the juice of one-half into a small bowl of water. Add the artichoke bottoms to the water as they are peeled to keep them from discoloring.

In a large skillet, heat 2 tablespoons of the olive oil over medium-high heat. Add the bread crumbs and cook, stirring constantly, until they are crisp, 2 to 3 minutes. Remove the bread crumbs from the skillet and set aside. Heat the remaining 2 tablespoons olive oil in the same skillet. Add

Continued on following page.

65

Continued from preceding page.

the onion and garlic; cook, stirring often, until they begin to soften, 3 to 5 minutes, watching closely so the garlic does not brown. Add the tomatoes, thyme, fish stock, vermouth and hot red pepper. Remove the artichokes from the water. Cut into 6 wedges each and add them to the skillet. Cover and bring to a boil. Reduce the heat to medium-low and simmer until the artichokes are tender, 12 to 15 minutes.

Arrange the clams atop the vegetable mixture in the skillet. Cover and cook over medium-high heat just until all the clams have opened, 3 to 5 minutes. Add the basil and season with salt and pepper to taste.

To serve, divide the linguine among 4 shallow soup or pasta bowls and top with a portion of the clams and sauce. Cut the other half of the lemon into wedges and add one to each bowl. Sprinkle with the bread crumbs and serve at once.

> *"In water one sees one's own face;*
> *But in wine one beholds the heart of another."*
> *--French Proverb*
>
> *(how romantic)*

Lobster with Red Wine Risotto

2 servings

RISOTTO:
1 c. dry red wine ☺
1/3 c. port ☺
1/4 c. unsalted butter
1 shallot, finely minced

1/2 c. rice
1 c. chicken stock, boiling
1/4 c. freshly-grated Parmesan
  cheese

SAUCE:
1 c. chicken stock, boiling
1/4 c. extra-virgin olive oil

1/2 c. freshly-grated Parmesan
  cheese
Ground white pepper

1 T. butter
2 (1 to 1 1/4 lb.) Maine lobsters,
  steamed, shells removed & meat
  cut into bite-size pieces

Shaved Parmesan cheese, for
  garnish
2 sprigs chervil, for garnish

In a saucepan set over high heat, bring the red wine and port to a boil. Reduce heat and simmer until reduced by half, about 5 minutes.

Set a heavy saucepan over medium heat, add the butter and cook the shallot, stirring, for 2 minutes. Add the rice and cook, stirring, for 2 minutes. Add the reduced wine and simmer until all the liquid is absorbed. Gently stirring while cooking, add about 1/4 cup of the chicken stock at a time, cooking until all the liquid is absorbed before adding more. Cook until the rice is al dente. Stir in the Parmesan cheese.

Continued on following page.

Continued from preceding page.

Sauce: Pour the hot stock into a blender and start blending on low, then gradually increase the speed to high. Slowly add the olive oil through the feeding tube; the sauce will look white and creamy. Add the cheese and mix just until blended. Season to taste with pepper. If the sauce is too thick, add a little more hot chicken stock.

To finish the dish, melt the butter in a small saucepan over medium heat and add the lobster meat and about 2 tablespoons water. Cook just until the lobster meat is warm, 2 to 3 minutes. Serve this in warmed, large, flat soup bowls. Place a mound of the risotto in the center, spoon a little of the creamy sauce around the risotto. Place the lobster on top and garnish with shaved Parmesan cheese and a sprig of chervil.

"How I see it is that men get one night of pleasure, and we get nine months of putting them through hell and getting away with it."
--Sara Swank

 Lobster Thermidor

4 servings

Expensive, rich and fabulous!

**2 lobsters, split, or 4 lobster tails,
  cooked
1/4 c. butter
1/3 c. flour
1 tsp. salt
1 tsp. minced onion
1 tsp. dry mustard
1/4 c. minced parsley
2 c. cream**

**1/2 c. sherry ☺
1 c. sautéed, sliced, fresh
  mushrooms or canned
  mushrooms
Pepper
Cayenne pepper
3 T. brandy ☺
1/4 c. grated Swiss cheese**

Dice lobster meat. Melt butter, blend in flour and add seasonings. Add cream and cook; stir to smooth sauce. Add sherry, mushrooms and pepper (better use white pepper if you have it, to avoid black specks). Heat lobster in sauce, adding brandy, and fill shells. Top with cheese. Broil until bobbing and serve hot. This dish may be put together several hours early and refrigerated. To heat, place the lobster in a 350° oven for 15 minutes, then under broiler just until tinged with brown.

*"I feel sorry for people who don't drink. When they wake up in the morning,
that's as good as they're going to feel all day."*
--Lyndon B. Johnson

69

Decadant Lobster and Vodka Sauce

4 servings

VODKA SAUCE:

2 T. butter	4 med. tomatoes, peeled, deseeded
2 c. yellow onions, chopped	& chopped
1 T. garlic, minced	2/3 c. good vodka ☺
1 tsp. salt	1 pt. heavy cream

Melt butter on medium-high in a skillet; sauté onions and garlic until golden. Stir in salt. Add tomatoes and vodka; cook until very thick. Pour cream into a saucepan and reduce on medium heat to a saucy consistency. Watch carefully not to burn.

LOBSTER TAIL:

4 (8 oz.) lobster tails	Vodka Sauce
2 T. butter	

Remove lobster meat from shells and cut into bite-size pieces. Sauté in butter until done. Drain excess liquid. Add Vodka Sauce. Serve over favorite cooked pasta.

"A man is incomplete until he is married. After that, he is finished."
--Zsa Zsa Gabor

Lobster Thermidor

6 servings

5 lobster tails, cut in chunks
2 T. tomato paste
4 T. brandy ☺
2 1/2 oz. sliced mushrooms
1/2 tsp. dry mustard
2 bay leaves

1/2 med. onion, chopped
1/3 btl. dry white wine ☺
1/2 pt. whipping cream
1/4 tsp. tarragon
Pinch of thyme
Dash of Tabasco sauce

Finely chop onions and sauté in oil in a heavy pot. Add tomato paste and simmer 3 minutes. Add pieces of lobster meat and sauté for a couple of minutes. Pour in wine and brandy and let simmer. To thicken, add 3 ounces of roux and whip over a low flame. Add cream and remaining ingredients and simmer, reducing to desired consistency. Serve either on rice, on a puff pastry or in the original lobster tail shell.

Variation: Shrimp and/or crabmeat may be substituted.

"Women are like cell phones. They like to be held and talked to,
but push the wrong button, and you'll be disconnected."
--Unknown

Savory Deviled Crabs

6 servings

Makes a delicious luncheon with crunchy green salad and hot rolls.

2 (6 oz.) pkg. frozen crab, thawed, or 2 (6 1/2 oz.) cans crabmeat
2 hard-cooked eggs, chopped
1 c. mayonnaise
1 tsp. minced onion
1 tsp. parsley
1 tsp. Worcestershire sauce
1 tsp. prepared mustard
2 tsp. lemon juice
1/2 tsp. salt
1/4 c. sherry ☺
1 c. buttered crumbs

Mix crabmeat, sherry, eggs, mayonnaise and seasonings. Fill 6 buttered ramekins and top with crumbs. Bake at 375° for 15 to 20 minutes. Or bake in a casserole 25 minutes.

"Wine rejoices the heart of man, and joy is the Mother of all virtue."
--Johann Wolfgang von Goethe

 Sherried Crabmeat

10 to 12 servings

1 c. chopped onion	4 pimentos, chopped
1 c. chopped green bell pepper	1 (8 oz.) jar sliced mushrooms,
1 c. chopped celery	drained
2 c. butter, divided	1/3 c. sherry (or more) ☺
3 lb. lump crabmeat	1 c. flour
1/2 c. chopped parsley	1 tsp. pepper
4 tsp. salt, divided	4 c. milk
2 tsp. Tabasco sauce	1/2 c. cracker crumbs
Juice of 2 lemons	

Preheat oven to 350°. Sauté onion, celery and green bell pepper in 1 cup butter until tender; remove from heat. In a large bowl, combine sautéed vegetables with crabmeat, parsley, 2 teaspoons salt, Tabasco sauce, lemon juice, pimentos, mushrooms and sherry. In a large double boiler, combine flour, pepper and remaining salt. Gradually stir in milk. Cook over hot water, stirring constantly, until mixture is smooth. Remove from heat and add remaining butter, stirring until melted. Combine sauce with crab mixture and spoon into a 4-quart baking dish. Sprinkle with cracker crumbs and bake for 30 minutes.

Note: Can be divided and baked in 2 (2-quart) baking dishes.

> *"Work is the curse of the drinking class."*
> *--Oscar Wilde*

73

Crab Cake with Mustard Sauce

4 servings

3 green onions, sliced	Salt & freshly-ground pepper
Olive oil	1 tsp. Dijon mustard
6 med. shrimp	Dash of Tabasco sauce
1 egg	3 dashes of Worcestershire sauce
1 c. whipping cream	1 c. crabmeat (jumbo lump)

SAUCE:

2 shallots, chopped	Salt & freshly-ground pepper
1/3 c. white wine ☺	1 tsp. Dijon mustard
2 T. whipping cream	1 tsp. chopped herbs (tarragon,
1/2 c. butter	chives, parsley)

Preheat oven to 350°. Cook on low heat, the sliced green onions in olive oil until soft. Process the shrimp in food processor for 30 seconds. Add egg and process again. Place bowl in freezer for 5 minutes. Add green onions; process. Add whipping cream and season lightly. Add mustard, Tabasco sauce and Worcestershire sauce. Fold in crabmeat.

In a nonstick saucepan, cook the crab cake in a ring (or shaped with a spoon) for 2 minutes on each side in oven.

Sauce: Reduce shallots and white wine to 1 tablespoon and add whipping cream. Reduce again to 1 tablespoon. Turn heat to very low. Whisk in butter, 1 tablespoon at a time. Season with salt, pepper and mustard. Add the chopped herbs.

Place crab cake in middle of plate and pour sauce around.

74

Panned Oysters

4 servings

These take just a minute to fix, they make a good late supper.

1 pt. lg. oysters	**Hot buttered toast or angel hair**
1/4 c. butter	**pasta**
1/3 c. dry white wine ☺	**Lemon quarters**
Salt & pepper	**Parsley**
	Dash of Worcestershire sauce

Drain oysters and heat in a skillet with butter until edges begin to curl. Add wine, salt and pepper, plus a dash of Worcestershire sauce, if you wish. Bring to simmering. Serve on hot toast or angel hair and garnish with lemon and parsley.

These are "pan roast" oysters. If you would rather, heat everything in a baking dish at 400° for 10 minutes.

"I had a rose named after me and I was very flattered. But I was not pleased to read the description in the catalog: 'No good in a bed, but fine against a wall.'"
--Eleanor Roosevelt

Mussels Marinière

4 servings

4 doz. mussels, well scrubbed & debearded
1/3 to 1/2 btl. white wine ☺
1 med. onion, finely-chopped
1 t. fresh lemon juice
1 tsp. salt

1 tsp. freshly-ground pepper
4 cloves garlic, finely-chopped
4 fresh basil leaves
3 parsley sprigs
4 T. butter
1 (16 oz.) can puréed tomatoes

Place mussels in large kettle with all ingredients, except butter and tomatoes. Bring to a boil and cook until mussels open. Discard any that do not open. Remove mussels. Add butter to liquid and reduce. Pass liquid through sieve lined with cheesecloth. Warm liquid with tomatoes. Pour over mussels, arrange in individual bowls.

Serve with crusty Italian or French bread.

*"Give me wine to wash me clean
from the weather-stains of care."*
--Ralph Waldo Emerson

Oysters and Crab

4 servings

Oysters poached in wine are delicious.

1 pt. lg. oysters
1 1/2 c. white wine ☺
1 T. lemon juice
2 T. butter
3 T. flour
1/2 c. cream

1/2 tsp. salt
1/8 tsp. white pepper
1/8 tsp. nutmeg
2 c. cooked shrimp or crabmeat, chopped
1/2 c. fine, dry bread crumbs

Poach the oysters gently in the wine and lemon juice until the edges begin to curl. Melt butter, stir in the flour, then the liquid in which oysters are poached. Cook, stirring constantly, until mixture thickens. Add cream and seasonings. Combine 1 cup of the sauce with the shrimp or crabmeat. Place in scallop shells or ramekins. Place several poached oysters on each portion and spoon sauce over oysters. Top with crumbs, dot with butter and brown quickly under broiler.

"Marriage is the triumph of imagination over intelligence.
Second marriage is the triumph of hope over experience."

Coquilles St. Jacques

6 servings

Very rich sauce!

3 lb. sm. scallops
1 T. minced shallots
1 1/4 c. flour
4 egg yolks
1 lb. fresh mushrooms

2 c. white wine ☺
1 stick butter
1 c. heavy cream
1 c. grated Swiss cheese
1 c. bread crumbs

Boil together shallots and wine. Add scallops and cook until scallops are done, about 3 minutes. Remove scallops and reserve liquid. Reduce liquid over high heat to 1 cup. In a saucepan, melt butter and add flour, a little bit at a time. After a few minutes of cooking, add the reserved, reduced scallop liquid. Simmer for 15 minutes. Add heavy cream mixed with egg yolks. Heat for 1 more minute. Add cheese and stir to melt. Sauté mushrooms over high heat in a small amount of butter. Drain and add to sauce. Add well-drained scallops back to sauce. Divide mixture into scallop shells. Sprinkle bread crumbs over top and put into very hot oven until bread crumbs begin to brown.

*"When a woman steals your husband, there is no better revenge
than to let her have him."*

⚕ Scallops and Shrimp in White Wine Sauce

6 to 8 servings

2 lb. shrimp, peeled & deveined	2 1/2 c. white wine ☺
2 T. shallots, chopped	2 T. lemon juice
1 T. butter	1 lb. mushrooms, sliced
3 T. butter, melted	3 T. flour
Salt & pepper, to taste	1 c. heavy cream
2 lb. scallops	1 c. Hollandaise sauce

Poach shrimp and scallops in the white wine with shallots and lemon juice. Drain the scallops and set aside. Put the poaching liquid in saucepan and boil. Sauté the mushrooms in 1 tablespoon of butter and add them to the shrimp and scallops. Mix the flour with the 3 tablespoons of melted butter and blend to a paste. Whip the paste into the boiling poaching liquid. Stir in the heavy cream. Cook for 5 minutes and season with salt and pepper. Add the Hollandaise sauce. Mix the sauce with the shrimp, scallops and mushrooms. Serve over rice pilaf.

"A word to the wise isn't necessary, it is the stupid ones who need all the advice."
--Bill Cosby

🍷 Broiled Shrimp with White Wine

4 to 5 servings

Delicious and so easy!

2 lb. raw shrimp, shelled & veined
1/4 c. melted butter
1 garlic clove, minced

1/4 c. dry white wine ☺
Salt & pepper

Toss shrimp in butter with garlic and wine to coat well. Broil about 5 minutes, 3 inches from heat. Season with salt and pepper.

🍷 Shrimp Scampi

2 to 4 servings

3/4 c. butter, room temp.
2 T. white wine ☺
2 cloves garlic, crushed
3 T. chopped fresh parsley
3 T. Parmesan cheese

Salt & freshly-ground pepper
3/4 lb. fresh shrimp, cleaned,
   deveined & butterflied
Fettuccine, cooked according to
   pkg. directions

Preheat oven to broil. Melt butter in shallow baking dish under broiler (watch to prevent burning). Remove from oven; stir in garlic, wine, parsley, Parmesan cheese, salt and pepper. Add shrimp and toss to cover. Place under broiler for 3 minutes; turn shrimp and broil another 3 to 4 minutes longer, or until shrimp is just opaque. Do not overcook.

Place fettuccine on a heated platter. Spoon shrimp mixture over top. Garnish with chopped fresh parsley and serve immediately.

Baked Stuffed Shrimp

4 servings

16 lg. shrimp, raw, cleaned,
  deveined & butterflied
20 butter-flavored crackers,
  crushed
1 (6 oz.) can crabmeat, drained
1/3 c. butter, melted

2 T. white wine ☺
1/4 c. chopped fresh parsley
2 cloves garlic, crushed
1/4 c. finely-chopped onion
1/4 c. finely-chopped green pepper

Preheat oven to 350°. Mix together cracker crumbs, crabmeat, butter, wine, parsley, garlic, onion and green pepper to make stuffing.

Arrange shrimp on ungreased baking pan. Spoon stuffing equally onto each shrimp. Bake for 20 to 25 minutes, or until shrimp is pink.

"Everyone has the ability of making someone happy,
some by entering the room, others by leaving it."
--Unknown

Prawns Sambuca Flambé

4 servings

Drink at your own risk while cooking.

4 oz. olive oil	1/4 c. fresh tomato, diced
1 T. fresh garlic, chopped	1 T. fresh tarragon, finely chopped
1 T. fresh shallots, chopped	2 tsp. salt & pepper
16 fresh prawns	4 oz. sweet butter
3 oz. Chardonnay or dry white wine ☺	16 oz. angel hair pasta, cooked
	Fresh tarragon leaves
2 oz. Sambuca liqueur ☺	2 chives

Heat oil in sauté pan; add garlic, shallots and prawns. Cook for 1 or 2 minutes. Add wine and Sambuca. Flambé.

Add tomatoes, tarragon, salt and pepper; cook for 2 more minutes. Add butter and reduce. Place over individual servings of pasta. Garnish with tarragon leaves and chives.

"Being a woman is a terribly difficult trade since it consists principally of dealing with men."
--Joseph Conrad
(Trade, Excuse me!) BJ

Seafood Risotto

4 to 6 servings

RISOTTO:
1/4 c. butter or margarine
1/2 c. olive oil
2 sm. onions, chopped

1 lb. Italian risotto
1/2 c. dry white wine ☺
8 c. chicken broth

SEAFOOD SAUCE:
1/4 c. butter or margarine
1/4 c. extra-virgin olive oil
1 onion, chopped
3 cloves garlic, chopped
3 (6 1/2 oz.) cans minced or
   chopped clams
1/2 c. chopped fresh parsley

1/4 tsp. oregano
1/2 c. dry white wine ☺
1 c. sliced mushrooms
Salt & freshly-ground pepper
1 lb. fresh shrimp, shelled &
   deveined or frozen shrimp,
   thawed & drained

Grated fresh Parmesan cheese

  Risotto: In separate large skillet, heat butter and olive oil. Sauté onion until golden. Stir in rice and cook for about 2 minutes. Add wine and cook for another 2 minutes. Heat chicken broth in saucepan. Begin adding broth to rice, 1/2 cup at a time. Continue adding broth until rice is soft in texture, approximately 15 minutes.

  Seafood Sauce: In a large skillet, heat butter and olive oil. Sauté onion and garlic until golden. Stir in clams with juice, parsley, oregano, wine and mushrooms. Simmer mixture 5 minutes. Season to taste with salt and pepper. Set aside.

  Bring seafood sauce to a boil, add shrimp and simmer for 4 minutes. Add seafood sauce mixture to risotto and continue heating for 1 to 2 minutes. Sprinkle cheese on top.

 Shrimp with Wild Rice

6 very generous servings

Not difficult. Better than you'd find in a restaurant!

1/2 lb. wild rice, washed & cooked in broth	1/2 lb. mushrooms, sliced
1 T. butter	2 T. butter
1 1/2 lb. shrimp, cooked, shelled & cleaned	1/2 c. Sauterne or other white table wine ☺
1 clove garlic, minced	1 can consommé, diluted with 1 can water
1/2 c. chopped onion	Salt & pepper
1 green pepper, chopped	1 T. cornstarch

Cook rice in 3 cups chicken broth or consommé about 25 minutes, or until tender, not stirring but lifting with a fork occasionally to prevent sticking. Rice should absorb all liquid and should not have to be drained. When tender, add butter to it. Sauté garlic, onion, green pepper and mushrooms in butter until lightly browned. Add wine and consommé and simmer gently for several minutes. Add salt and pepper as needed. Mix cornstarch to a paste with a little water and stir into sauce. Cook until thickened, stirring constantly. Place prepared shrimp on a bed of the wild rice in a casserole; pour sauce over them and bake 15 minutes at 375°.

 Special Shrimp Curry

4 servings

1/3 c. butter
1 med. onion, minced
2 stalks celery, minced
1 carrot, scraped & grated
1 tart apple, peeled, cored & grated
2 T. chopped parsley
1 T. curry powder

1/2 c. flour
3 c. chicken stock or bouillon
1/2 c. cream or evaporated milk
4 T. sherry ☺
Salt, to taste
1 1/2 lb. cooked shrimp, peeled &
   cleaned

Melt butter in top of large double boiler over direct heat; add onion, celery, carrot, apple and parsley. Sauté gently 5 minutes. Blend in curry powder and flour. Add chicken stock and cream; cook slowly, stirring constantly, until mixture boils and thickens. Add sherry, salt and shrimp. Place over hot water in double boiler. Cover and cook 20 to 30 minutes before serving on rice with chutney, chopped cashews and any other curry condiments you may want. Put in a chafing dish and serve.

"Some people are alive only because it is illegal to kill them."
--Unknown

Shrimp A la Mann

4 servings

1 lb. raw jumbo shrimp, peeled
2 T. soft butter
1 T. finely-minced parsley
1 sliver garlic, mashed
2 T. dry sherry ☺
1/4 tsp. Worcestershire sauce

1 T. fine, dry bread crumbs
About 6 slices bacon, cut in half
1 c. wild rice, cooked tender in 3 c.
   clear chicken broth, well
   seasoned

Make a deep cut in each shrimp when you remove the vein down the back, to hold the filling. Cream together the butter, parsley, garlic, wine, Worcestershire sauce and bread crumbs. Fill the tunnels in the shrimp. Wrap each shrimp in a half slice of bacon and broil until bacon is crisp. Then bed the shrimp on the wild rice on a heatproof platter and heat 2 or 3 minutes in a hot oven, 450°, to blend the flavors.

"Guys who have big muscles and a nice car
are usually trying to make up for a lost feature."
--Unknown

♀ Shrimp in Tomato Cream Sauce

4 servings

1 T. olive oil
1/2 c. minced sweet onion
4 cloves garlic, peeled & minced
1/2 c. sweet red wine ☺
6 roma tomatoes, or 3 med. tomatoes, chopped
1/2 tsp. dried oregano, crushed to release flavor
1/4 tsp. dried basil
1 c. heavy cream, or cream & milk combined

1 lb. lg. raw shrimp (31 to 40 count), peeled & deveined
1 T. chopped fresh parsley
1/4 c. grated Parmesan cheese
Salt & freshly-ground pepper, to taste
Angel hair pasta, cooked al dente, or tortellini
Additional chopped fresh parsley, for garnish

Heat a large, heavy skillet over medium heat. Add olive oil and sauté shallots or sweet onions for 2 minutes. Add garlic and sauté another minute. Carefully pour in red wine and cook another minute, stirring constantly. Add chopped tomatoes, oregano and basil, stirring to combine. Simmer about 5 minutes for flavors to blend.

Add heavy cream to tomato mixture. Continue cooking until reduced and somewhat thickened. Add shrimp and parsley to tomato cream sauce and simmer, turning often, only until pink and opaque. (Do not overcook.) Stir in Parmesan cheese, salt and pepper to taste. Serve immediately over cooked angel hair pasta.

Seafood Supreme

12 servings

Great for large dinner parties.

1/2 c. butter or margarine	**Salt & pepper**
1/2 c. flour	**4 c. diced cooked or canned**
2 c. chicken stock or canned broth	**lobster, shrimp, crabmeat, diced**
or bouillon made from cubes	**(1 or all 3)**
1 c. cream	**1 (8 oz.) can mushroom stems &**
6 oz. pimento cream cheese	**pieces, drained**
1/2 c. sherry or a white table	
wine ☺	

Melt butter and stir in flour; add chicken stock and cream. Cook, stirring constantly, until mixture boils and thickens. Add cheese and sherry; stir over low heat until cheese melts. Season with salt and pepper. Add seafood and mushrooms. Heat gently just until piping hot. Serve over mounds of hot cooked rice.

The mixture may be prepared ahead of time and reheated just before serving in a chafing dish, the top of a double boiler, or over low heat.

"The law of heredity is that all undesirable traits come from the other parent."
--Unknown

Poultry

FAVORITE RECIPES
FROM MY COOKBOOK

Recipe Name	Page Number

 Fruit-Glazed Roast Chicken

4 servings

1 (3 1/2 lb.) whole frying chicken	1 c. dry white wine, divided ☺
Salt & freshly-ground pepper	3/4 c. apricot, pineapple or peach
1/4 c. water	preserves or jam

Preheat oven to 350°. Butter 9x9-inch glass baking dish and line the bottom with parchment paper. (Do not substitute foil or waxed paper for parchment paper.)

Rinse and dry chicken. Season inside with salt and pepper. Fold wings under back and tie legs together. Place breast-side down (yes, I said upside-down and no I haven't been drinking) in prepared baking dish. Mix 1/2 cup wine and water together, and pour over chicken. Bake for 45 minutes, basting occasionally with juices. Turn chicken breast-side up and continue to bake and baste for another 45 minutes.

Mix the preserves and remaining 1/2 cup wine in a small saucepan and bring to simmering. Brush generously over the chicken every 5 minutes during the last 15 minutes of baking.

Carve and serve hot.

"The sincerest love is the love of food."
--Bernard Shaw
(And wine!) BJ

89

Chicken Breasts with Ginger

4 to 6 servings

8 chicken breasts, boned with skin
   intact
Flour
Salt & freshly-ground pepper
1/4 c. butter
2 T. oil
1 tsp. ground ginger

1 tsp. curry powder
1/4 c. chopped crystallized ginger
1/2 c. chicken broth
1/3 c. white wine ☺
1/2 c. orange juice
2 T. brown sugar

   Preheat oven to 350°. Dredge chicken breasts with flour, salt and pepper. Melt butter in large sauté pan. Add oil, ground ginger and curry powder. Let mixture boil for 20 seconds. Add chicken breasts, and sauté for 5 minutes on each side. Place in baking dish. Sprinkle chicken with crystallized ginger. To the butter mixture left in the pan, add chicken broth, wine, orange juice and brown sugar. Simmer for 5 to 10 minutes. Pour over chicken and bake 8 minutes. Just before serving, put chicken under broiler for 2 minutes, or more if necessary, to crisp and glaze skin.

"Men should be like Kleenex...soft, strong and disposable."
--Mrs. White, Clue
(Yes!) BJ

 Chicken Cacciatora

4 or 5 servings

1 (2 1/2 to 3 1/2 lb.) chicken, in
  pieces
1/2 c. olive oil
1 slice onion
1 minced clove garlic
1 (1 lb. 2 oz.) can Italian pear
  tomatoes

1 1/2 tsp. salt
1/4 tsp. pepper
1/2 c. red wine (Chianti would be
  great) ☺
Chopped parsley

Brown the chicken pieces in the oil; reduce heat, add onion and garlic and sauté until onion is yellow. Drain excess oil. Add tomatoes and seasonings; simmer until chicken is tender and tomatoes are reduce to a thick sauce, about 45 minutes. Taste and add more seasonings if you need them. Add wine the last 15 minutes. Sprinkle with parsley when you've turned the chicken onto a hot platter.

For a special party, add 1/4 pound finely-diced ham and 1/2 pound sliced fresh mushrooms. Sauté both with chicken and seasoning. Mushrooms alone may be added.

"Wine, madam, is God's next best gift to man."
--Ambrose Bierce, "The Devil's Dictionary," 1907
(Was golf the first?) BJ

Chicken Marengo

6 servings

2 broiler-fryer chickens, cut up	**1 c. white table wine** ☺
1/4 c. olive oil	**Bouquet garni***
Salt & pepper	**1 clove garlic, chopped fine**
2 T. flour	**1 T. tomato paste**
1/2 c. stock or water	**1/2 lb. mushrooms, sliced**

Brown chicken in the oil and season with salt and pepper. Remove chicken from pan. Stir in flour and add stock and wine. When well blended, add bouquet garni, garlic, tomato paste and mushrooms. Season with more salt and pepper. Add chicken, and coat each piece with sauce. Cover and simmer for 30 minutes, remove herbs and serve.

*Bouquet garni is commonly used in French cooking. It consists of 3 or 4 sprigs of parsley, a sprig of thyme and a small bay leaf tied together. The thyme should be surrounded by the parsley so that the little leaves will not float into the sauce. You may substitute 1/4 teaspoon powdered thyme and 1 teaspoon parsley flakes, but tie these in a cheesecloth bag or strain sauce before serving.

"Wine makes daily living easier, less hurried,
with fewer tensions and more tolerance."
--Benjamin Franklin
(One man got it right.) BJ

Hawaiian Chicken for a Party

12 servings

This casserole can be fixed a day early.

2 stewing chickens, about 4 1/2 lb. each	3 1/2 c. coconut water & chicken stock
1 sm. fresh coconut	2/3 c. sherry ☺
1 fresh pineapple	2 T. chopped preserved ginger
1/2 c. butter	1 c. chopped macadamia nuts,
1/2 c. flour	cashews or toasted slivered almonds

Simmer the cut-up chickens in water to cover, with 1 1/2 tablespoons salt, juice of 1 lemon, a cluster of celery tops, a few peppercorns and a bay leaf. Cool in stock. Remove meat from bones and dice or slice. Strain stock; chill and remove fat. Bore holes in 2 eyes of the coconut, drain water and combine with stock to make 3 1/2 cups of liquid. Grate coconut meat. Slice, pare and core pineapple and cut slices into small piece: quarter the slices, then slice the quartered pieces very thin. Melt butter, blend in flour and gradually add stock and coconut water, stirring until thickened. Add sherry and ginger, and more salt and pepper if needed. Arrange alternate layers of chicken, grated coconut, pineapple, nuts and sauce in baking dish. Bake half an hour at 375°.

Cheese or buttered crumbs may be used as a topping.

Peruvian Chicken

4 to 6 servings

Your friends will beg for this recipe!

1 (about 3 lb.) chicken, cut up, or 8 to 12 pieces of chicken
3 T. butter
1 sm. onion, minced
6 whole cloves, or 1/8 tsp. ground
1 bay leaf
1/2 tsp. cumin seasoning, or 1/4 tsp. cumin seed

1 c. concentrated stock, or canned consommé
1 c. white port ☺
1/2 c. raisins
1/2 c. shredded blanched almonds
1/2 c. heavy cream
2 egg yolks
1/3 c. more wine ☺
Salt & pepper

Brown chicken in butter; add onion last few minutes. Add cloves, bay leaf, cumin and stock. Cover and simmer gently. Add port, raisins and almonds when about half-cooked. Simmer until tender, then mix cream, egg yolks and wine. Stir in a little of the hot sauce, and pour into the chicken. Stir until thickened, about a minute. Don't let sauce boil. Add salt and pepper if necessary.

"When you're in jail, a good friend will be trying to bail you out.
A best friend will be in the cell next to you saying, 'Damn, that was fun.'"
--Unknown

♇ Arroz Con Pollo

8 or more servings

A Latin American special dish.

2 (about 3 lb.) chickens, or 16
  pieces chicken
Flour, salt & pepper, for coating
6 shallots or green onions, sliced
2 med. onions, sliced thin
1 clove garlic, minced
1/2 c. hot oil
4 to 6 fresh tomatoes, peeled

2 green peppers, diced
2 c. chicken broth (from necks,
  backs, giblets)
1 rounded teaspoon saffron
1 to 2 tsp. salt (taste to be sure)
2 c. uncooked rice
1/2 c. sherry ☺

In a large skillet, sauté onions and garlic in oil in a large skillet. Remove from pan and brown chicken pieces (I use just legs, breasts, wings, 16 pieces) after coating with seasoned flour. Return onions to skillet and slice in tomatoes and peppers. Add broth and saffron. Cover and simmer until nearly tender, about an hour. Then add the rice and cook 30 minutes, or so longer, until rice is tender and has absorbed moisture. Mixture should be rather dry. Finish with sherry.

"Who took the cork out of the lunch?"
--W. C. Fields
(A man after my own heart!)

95

Chicken Flambé with Brandied Cherry Sauce

A special dinner for 2.

2 (8 oz.) chicken breasts with bone & skin
1 oz. melted butter
1 tsp. paprika

3 to 4 T. brandy ☺
1 pinch of salt & white pepper, to taste

BING CHERRY SAUCE:
1 (8 oz.) can black bing cherries
2 T. Burgundy wine ☺
2 T. sugar

1/2 tsp. cornstarch
1 pinch of salt

Bing Cherry Sauce: Drain juice from cherries. Combine juice with sugar, cornstarch and salt; mix thoroughly. Bring mixture to a boil until sauce thickens. Add the drained cherries and Burgundy; cook until it thickens. Do not boil wine.

Season chicken breasts with salt, white pepper, paprika, and brush with butter. Bake for 30 minutes at 325°, or until cooked and tender. Place chicken in a medium-size ovenproof serving dish and cover with sauce. Have table set, candles lit, all accompaniments on table, and turn off lights when ready to flambé.

How to flambé: Pour 1/4 ounce or 1 to 2 tablespoons of brandy over dish and place in middle of table. Using long wooden matches, ignite chicken breast. When flame goes out and liquor has burned off, you are ready to serve.

🍷 Chicken Baked in Foil

4 servings

Great on a grill, too!

2 1/2 to 3 lb. chicken, quartered	**1/2 tsp. pepper**
Oil, for browning	**1/2 tsp. paprika**
1 doz. mushrooms	**1 tsp. chopped parsley**
1 doz. sm. white onions	**1/2 c. white table wine** ☺
1 tsp. salt	

Brown chicken quarters lightly in oil. Sauté onions and mushrooms. Tear from a roll of aluminum foil, 12 inches wide, 4 pieces, each 14 inches long. Butter center of each. Set a quarter of chicken, 3 onions and 3 mushroom caps on each, then season with the salt, pepper, paprika and parsley. Pour 2 tablespoons wine over each portion. Bring edges of foil up over chicken and double fold to make it tight. Set packets on a cookie sheet and bake an hour at 425°. (You need a hotter than usual oven because of the foil insulation.) Turn oven down to warm to hold chicken until you are ready to serve it. It waits nicely for your friends.

"Sorrow can be alleviated by good sleep, a bath and a glass of good wine. "
--St. Thomas Aquinas
(And sometimes a half dozen chocolate chip cookies!) BJ

Chicken Pie

6 servings

FILLING AND SAUCE:

1 whole lg. chicken
Salt
Pepper
Bay leaf
1/2 c. butter
1/2 c. flour

4 c. chicken stock
3 T. white wine ☺
1 pt. half & half
Dashes of Tabasco &
  Worcestershire sauce
Egg wash (see recipe below)

  Boil chicken until meat is ready to fall off the bone. Let cool. Pick meat off and dice; set aside. Put all remaining chicken parts back in water. Add seasonings (salt, pepper, bay leaf, etc.). Simmer for a few hours, strain.

  Melt butter in a saucepan over medium heat and add flour. Stir until smooth; add stock and a splash of white wine. Cook and stir until thickened. Lower heat and add half & half and stir until smooth. Add Tabasco sauce and Worcestershire sauce. Mix. Add half of the sauce to chicken meat and fill the pie shell. Cover with second pie dough sheet. Crimp edges and cut slits in top to vent.

  Mix 1 egg white with 1 tablespoon of water. Brush egg wash on top crust. Bake at 350° until golden brown.

  Yield: 1 pie.

PIE DOUGH:

  Makes one 10-inch double-crust pie. Or use the refrigerated pie dough. Works fine and speeds things up.

2 1/2 c. flour
3/4 c. butter

1 egg
3 T. sour cream

  Mix flour and butter; press until crumbly. Add the egg and sour cream, but keep coarse. Roll pie dough out in 2 sheets. Grease a 10-inch pie pan and line with 1 sheet. Reserve second sheet (see above).

  Note: I double it and freeze one.

Coq au Vin

4 servings

1 T. olive oil
2 carrots, chopped
1 med. onion, chopped
1 (10 oz.) pkg. sliced mushrooms
2 garlic cloves, crushed
2 lb. sm. bone-in chicken thighs,
  skin removed
2 slices bacon

1 c. dry red wine ☺
3 T. brandy ☺
3 T. all-purpose flour
1 can chicken broth (1 3/4 c.)
1/4 tsp. salt
3 T. chopped fresh parsley leaves,
  for garnish

In nonstick skillet, heat oil over medium-high heat until hot. Add carrot, onion and mushrooms; cook 15 minutes, or until vegetables are lightly browned, stirring. Add garlic and cook 30 minutes, stirring often. Remove skillet from heat.

Meanwhile, heat nonstick 5 to 6-quart Dutch oven over medium-high heat until hot. Add chicken and bacon; cook 12 to 13 minutes, or until chicken is tender and golden, turning chicken over halfway through cooking time. When bacon is browned, transfer to paper towels to drain. Crumble when cool. Stir wine and brandy into Dutch oven with chicken; heat to boiling. Boil 1 minute.

In 2-quart liquid measuring cup, with wire whisk or fork, mix flour with broth until blended. Add broth mixture, salt and mushroom mixture to Dutch oven; heat to boiling over medium-high heat. Reduce heat to medium; cook 5 minutes, or until chicken is cooked through. Sprinkle with crumbled bacon, and garnish with parsley.

Vermouth Chicken Scallopine

4 to 6 servings

2 lb. chicken breasts, skinned & boned	2 to 3 cloves garlic, crushed
Salt & freshly-ground pepper	6 green onions, minced
Flour	1/2 c. vermouth ☺
1/4 c. olive oil, divided	2 T. fresh lime juice
	Parsley sprigs, for garnish

Place chicken between 2 sheets of waxed paper and flatten to 1/8-inch with a steak mallet (great if you're mad about something). Season with salt and pepper. Dredge in flour. Heat skillet and add 2 tablespoons oil, when hot, sauté garlic and onion 1 minute; remove and reserve.

Heat another 2 or more tablespoons oil. When hot, sauté chicken on both sides until browned, add more oil if necessary. Remove chicken from skillet and keep warm. Return onion and garlic to skillet and add vermouth and lemon juice; bring to boil and reduce slightly. Season with salt and pepper.

Arrange chicken on platter and spoon sauce on top. Garnish with sprigs of fresh parsley and serve immediately.

The vermouth makes this dish great!

"When a man drinks wine, he begins to be better pleased with himself."
--Plato
(Lord, help us!) BJ

Chicken Stir-Fry

4 servings

1 c. buttermilk baking mix
1 tsp. pepper
1 1/2 lb. uncooked, diced chicken
2 eggs, slightly beaten
1 T. canola oil or vegetable oil
4 med. carrots, thinly-sliced
8 morel mushrooms, diced
1 green pepper, chopped & diced

1 Vidalia onion, diced
2 T. water
3 T. olive oil
1 c. dry white wine ☺
2 T. teriyaki sauce
2 c. hot cooked white or brown
  rice

In large plastic bag, combine mix and peppers; shake to mix. Set aside. Mix chicken meat and eggs; coat well. Pour chicken in bag and shake to coat well with mixture. In a wok or large skillet, heat 1 tablespoon oil over medium-high heat. Then add carrots to cook and stir for 1 to 3 minutes. Add green pepper and onion; cook for another minute. Add water and cover; steam 2 to 3 minutes, until vegetables are desired tenderness. Remove vegetable from skillet. Add remaining oil to skillet and add chicken. Cook and stir until chicken is golden brown and no pink remains in the middle. Combine wine and teriyaki sauce; pour over meat. Return vegetables to skillet and stir until heated through. Serve with hot rice.

"No matter how happily a woman may be married, it always pleases
her to discover that there is a nice man who wishes she were not."
--H. L. Mencken

Chicken Breasts with Leeks and Pine Nuts
(Can also use Pork Chops or Pork Tenderloin)

4 servings

4 T. pine nuts
2 T. extra-virgin olive oil
4 (6 oz.) chicken breast halves,
  with skin
2 med. leeks, white and tender
  green parts, halved lengthwise &
  chopped

2 med. shallots, sliced thin
1 1/2 c. chicken stock (can use
  chicken broth)
1 c. dry white wine
  (Chardonnay) ☺
4 T. cold, unsalted butter, cut into
  sm. pieces

Preheat oven to 300°. In skillet, toast the pine nuts over moderately high heat, stirring until golden brown (about 2 minutes). Put on small plate.

Use same skillet; heat the oil. Season chicken breasts with salt and pepper and add to skillet, skin-side down. Cook, turning once, and press with a spatula, until browned on both sides (about 5 to 6 minutes). Put chicken breasts on a large rimmed baking sheet and cook for about 20 minutes, or until just white in center.

While chicken is cooking, add leeks and shallots to skillet and cook over low heat, stirring, for about 7 minutes, or until soft. Add the wine; increase heat to high. Boil until reduced by half (takes 3 to 4 minutes). Add chicken stock and boil until reduced to 1/2 cup (about 8 to 10 minutes). Remove the skillet from the heat and add the butter, 1 tablespoon at a time. Season sauce with salt and pepper. Put chicken on plates, pour on the sauce and the pine nuts to the top. Serve.

Open a bottle of your favorite white wine and enjoy!

Easy Chicken Piccata

4 servings

4 chicken breast cutlets (about
  1 1/2 lb.)
1 T. all-purpose flour
1/2 tsp. onion powder
1/2 tsp. garlic powder
1/2 tsp. sea salt or kosher salt
1/4 tsp. freshly-ground black
  pepper

2 T. olive oil
1 T. butter
1/3 c. white wine ☺
1 T. lemon juice (about 1/2 lemon)
1/2 c. chicken stock
1 T. sm. capers, drained

Combine flour, onion powder, garlic powder, kosher salt and black pepper. Sprinkle evenly on both sides of chicken cutlets.

Heat a large, heavy skillet over medium heat until hot. Add the olive oil and swirl to coat the bottom of the pan. Add the chicken in one layer, and cook on the first side for 5 minutes, until golden brown. Turn the chicken cutlets to the second side; add butter, white wine and lemon juice, swirling around chicken to combine; cook about 1 minute. Add chicken stock and capers; cook another 1 to 2 minutes, until chicken is no longer pink in center (internal temperature should be 170°) and pan gravy has thickened.

Serve with piccata sauce over the top of the chicken cutlets.

Great with couscous.

Gruyére and Chicken Roulade

4 servings

4 chicken breasts, skinned &
  boned
4 lean smoked ham slices
4 Gruyére cheese slices
1/4 c. chopped chives

2 T. olive oil
1 garlic clove, crushed
1/3 c. white wine ☺
Salt & pepper, to taste
2/3 c. whipping cream

Preheat oven to 350°.

Slice 3/4 of the way, horizontally, through the chicken breasts, cutting through the rounded edge. Open out, cover with plastic wrap and beat with a rolling pin to flatten (anger management!). Cover each chicken fillet with a ham slice, then a Gruyére slice. Set aside 1 tablespoon chives; sprinkle rest over cheese. Roll up chicken like a jellyroll, and secure with wooden picks or string.

In an ovenproof pan, heat oil. Cook chicken rolls gently, turning occasionally or until sealed. Pour off excess oil. Add garlic, wine and seasoning to pan. Cover and bake 25 to 30 minutes, or until tender. Place roulades on a dish; remove wooden picks or string and keep warm.

Put pan on high heat and boil rapidly to reduce contents slightly. Add cream and reserved chives and heat through.

Cut each chicken roulade into 1/2-inch slices and arrange them overlapping on 4 warmed dinner plates. Top with sauce and serve immediately, with a selection of cooked baby vegetables.

♈ Quick Couscous with Chicken

6 to 8 servings

1 (3 lb.) chicken, cut into serving pieces
Salt & pepper, to taste
2 T. cooking oil
1 onion, sliced
1 lg. carrot, diced
3 garlic cloves, minced
1 can peeled, whole plum tomatoes, drained & chopped (about 1 lb. fresh tomatoes)
1 tsp. ground cumin
1 tsp. ground allspice
2 c. chicken broth or vegetable stock, divided

1/2 c. dry white wine ☺
1/2 tsp. dried red chili flakes, or other hot pepper sauce
2 sm. zucchini, diced
3 T. tomato paste
1 (15 oz.) can cooked garbanzos (chick peas), rinsed & drained
4 T. chopped fresh cilantro, or 3 T. chopped fresh parsley, divided
1 T. butter
1 1/2 c. quick-cooking or "instant" couscous
Liquid pepper sauce

Rinse chicken, pat dry, and season with salt and pepper. Heat oil in large casserole or Dutch oven; brown chicken and remove. Add onion, carrot and garlic; sauté until softened. Add tomatoes, cumin and allspice; cook for 5 minutes, stirring. Stir in 1/2 cup chicken broth, wine and red chili flakes, and return chicken to casserole. Cover and simmer 15 minutes. Add zucchini, and simmer until chicken is tender (20 to 30 minutes more). Stir in tomato paste; add garbanzos and half the chopped cilantro or parsley, heat through.

While chicken is simmering, bring remaining chicken broth (and butter if you are using it) to a boil and add couscous; stir well. Cover and remove from heat. Let couscous stand 5 minutes, fluff with fork, and spoon onto serving platter. Arrange chicken and vegetables around it. Pour some sauce over top, and garnish with remaining cilantro or parsley.

♉ Chicken with Vermouth, Mushrooms and Onions

1 (2 1/2 to 3 lb.) chicken, cut up &
  skinned, if desired
Canola oil
1/2 c. vermouth ☺
1 onion, sliced

1 lb. mushrooms, cleaned &
  halved
2 garlic cloves, crushed
1 c. Chardonnay ☺
1 tsp. dried tarragon
Salt & pepper

Brown chicken over medium-high heat in heavy, nonstick frying pan (or use a little canola oil). Turn to brown on all sides. Add vermouth, onion, mushrooms and garlic. Bring to boil, then gradually add Chardonnay. Stir in tarragon, salt and pepper, cover, reduce heat. Let simmer about 50 minutes, until chicken is 165° (it will continue to cook after removing from heat).

"Mobile phones are the only subject on which
men boast about who's got the smallest."
--Neil Kinnock
(That's ok, we women will discuss the other!)

Chicken 'N Potato Bake

4 boneless chicken breasts
1/2 c. sherry ☺
4 med. potatoes, prebaked, not
  peeled
1 clove garlic
1 med. onion
8 oz. fresh mushrooms, sliced

1 bag frozen California Blend
  frozen vegetables, thawed &
  drained
1/2 to 3/4 c. ranch salad dressing
  (lite is ok to use)
1 to 2 c. shredded Colby-Jack
  cheese

In a small amount of oil, sauté chicken breasts with garlic and onions. Add sherry and mushrooms; simmer until mushrooms are tender.

Cut baked potatoes into bite-size pieces and put on bottom of 9x13-inch casserole dish. Drain chicken mixture and add next. Pour ranch dressing over the top and add the vegetables. Last, sprinkle on the cheese. Cover with foil (you could freeze the dish at this time for baking later); bake at 350° until heated through, about 45 minutes. If frozen, increase baking time to 1 1/2 hours.

Make sure you use the no-stick foil or spray your foil with Pam.

"I don't plan to grow old gracefully.
I plan to have face-lifts until my ears meet."
--Rita Rudner
(A woman after my own heart!!!) BJ

♈ Chicken, Sausage and Black Olives

6 servings

Sounds weird, but good!

**4 Italian sausages with fennel
  (sweet or hot)**
2 T. olive oil
3 cloves garlic, finely-chopped
6 boneless chicken breast halves
2/3 c. dry white wine ☺
1 green pepper, sliced in strips
1 red pepper, sliced in strips
1 c. sliced fresh mushrooms

1 sweet onion, coarsely-chopped
**1/4 c. chopped fresh oregano, or
  1 1/2 T. dried**
**2 T. chopped fresh tarragon, or 1 T.
  dried**
 **Salt & freshly-ground black
  pepper, to taste**
1/2 c. chopped black olives
Hot cooked rice

Brown Italian sausages in heavy skillet. Remove and cut in bite-size pieces. Add olive oil to skillet and sauté garlic about 2 minutes, being careful not to burn it. Sprinkle salt on chicken. Brown chicken in garlic oil about 5 minutes on each side. Remove and keep warm.

Add white wine to skillet and scrape up all clinging bits in pan. Heat about 2 minutes. Add chicken, Italian sausages, sweet peppers (both colors), mushrooms and sweet onion. Stir in oregano, tarragon, freshly-ground black pepper and olives. Cover and simmer 20 to 30 minutes, or until chicken is tender. Taste and adjust seasonings. Serve over hot cooked rice.

 Chicken Cacciatore

4 servings

MARINARA SAUCE:

1/4 c. olive oil
6 to 8 cloves garlic, chopped
1 tsp. chopped fresh parsley
2 T. chopped fresh basil

1/2 tsp. crushed red pepper flakes
2 (28 oz.) cans whole Italian
 tomatoes, or use fresh tomatoes

CHICKEN:

1 (4 lb.) whole chicken, or get pick
 of the chick (saves time &
 energy)
Salt & black pepper, to taste
1/4 c. olive oil (do not use extra-
 virgin olive oil)
1 med. onion, thinly-sliced
3 cloves garlic, sliced

1/2 c. dry sherry ☺
2 to 4 c. Marinara Sauce from
 above
1/2 to 3/4 lb. sliced fresh
 mushrooms
15 to 20 pitted olives (kalamata
 olives work great)
4 fresh basil leaves, chopped

Marinara Sauce: Heat the oil in a large saucepan over medium heat. Add the garlic and cook until soft. Add the parsley, basil and red pepper flakes and heat to release flavors, about 10 seconds. Drain the liquid from the canned tomatoes and reserve. Crush the tomatoes with your hands and add to the garlic mixture. Add the reserved juice and bring to a simmer. Simmer gently for 30 to 40 minutes, but do not let the sauce reduce or overcook. Refrigerate until needed.
 Yield: 6 cups.

Continued on following page.

109

Continued from preceding page.

Chicken: Cut the chicken into 8 pieces and season with salt and pepper. Over medium-high heat, heat the olive oil in a skillet large enough to hold the chicken pieces without crowding. When the oil is hot, carefully add the chicken pieces. Brown the chicken on both sides and remove from the pan. Add the onion and cook for 1 to 2 minutes, or until soft. Add the garlic and cook for 1 minute more. Drain off the oil and add the chicken back to the pan. Add the sherry and cook over high heat, scraping any browned bits from the bottom of the pan, until reduced by half.

Add 2 cups of the Marinara Sauce. Use 4 cups if needing extra sauce for a side dish of pasta (freeze any remaining sauce). Reduce heat and gently simmer for about 30 minutes, turning chicken pieces once or twice. Add the mushrooms, olives and basil; continue simmering for 15 minutes more. Turn off heat and let rest for 15 minutes. Skim fat from the surface. Taste and adjust seasoning. Serve hot.

"A woman knows all about her children. She knows about dentist appointments, soccer games, romances, best friends, location of friend's houses, favorite foods, secret fears and hopes and dreams. A man is vaguely aware of some short people living in the house."
--Unknown

110

Chicken with Red Wine and Mustard

4 servings

**4 trimmed boneless, skinless
chicken breasts, tenderloin
removed & cooked separately, or
saved for another use**
**Kosher salt & freshly-ground
black pepper**

Flour, for dredging
**Ingredients for pan sauce (see the
recipes below)**
3 T. unsalted butter
1 T. vegetable or olive oil

Season the chicken breasts on both sides with ample salt and pepper. Put a handful of flour in a pie pan or other sided plate and position it near the stove. Combine the sauce ingredients (see options below) of your choice in a 1-cup Pyrex measuring cup or small bowl.

Heat 2 tablespoons of the butter and the oil in a large skillet over medium heat. Dredge one of the chicken breasts in the flour, coating both sides well but shaking off any excess. Increase the heat of the pan to medium-high.

Before adding the chicken, test the heat of the pan by flicking in a little of the dredging flour. If the flour sizzles enthusiastically and immediately turns golden, the pan is ready. Add the first floured chicken breast. Then quickly flour the remaining breasts and add them to the pan. Cook for about 4 minutes without moving the breasts. Then, starting with the first one in the pan, turn them over and cook for another 3 to 4 minutes on the other side.

Transfer the chicken to a plate or plates and keep it warm. Add the pan sauce ingredients to the hot pan and boil, stirring and scraping up the browned bits in the bottom of the pan, over high heat until the liquid is

Continued on following page.

Continued from preceding page.

reduced by half. Add the remaining tablespoon of butter and whisk until smooth and glossy. (Tilt the pan to bring the small amount of liquid to one side while you whisk in the butter.) Spoon the sauce over the chicken and serve immediately.

RED WINE AND MUSTARD:

1/4 c. low-salt chicken stock   1 tsp. Dijon mustard
1/3 c. red wine ☺

Or try these sauces!

PORT WITH DRIED CHERRIES:

2/3 c. port wine ☺   2 tsp. seedless raspberry jam
2 T. dried cherries or cranberries

LEMON-CAPER:

6 T. low-salt chicken stock   2 tsp. drained capers
2 T. lemon juice   1 tsp. white wine ☺

VERMOUTH WITH PRUNES:

8 T. sweet vermouth ☺   1/4 c. chopped prunes
2 T. cider vinegar

TOMATO-TARRAGON:

1/4 c. low-salt chicken stock   4 canned tomatoes, seeded &
1/3 c. dry white wine ☺   chopped
1 tsp. minced fresh tarragon

Chicken and Ham Imperial

6 servings

Easy.

1/2 c. butter
1/2 c. flour
1 qt. milk
1/2 lb. fresh mushrooms, sliced &
  sautéed in 3 T. butter
4 c. diced cooked chicken & ham,
  any proportion

2/3 c. sherry ☺
2 c. grated sharp Cheddar cheese
2 tsp. minced onion
2 tsp. salt (taste to be sure)
1 tsp. freshly-ground black pepper
1/2 c. slivered toasted almonds
  (opt.)

Melt butter in saucepan or chafing dish. Blend in flour; add milk and stir to smooth sauce. Add mushrooms, chicken and ham, sherry, cheese, onion and seasonings. Stir thoroughly and heat until bubbly. Sprinkle with almonds. Serve over hot rice.

"I'm like old wine. They don't bring me out very often, but I'm well preserved."
--Rose Kennedy (1890-1995) On her 100th birthday, 1991
(We women just get better with age.) BJ

🍷 Creamy Chicken Marsala

1/4 c. olive oil
3 garlic cloves
Flour, for dredging
3 whole chicken breasts, halved
1/2 lb. fresh mushrooms, sliced

1 1/2 c. Marsala wine ☺
1 1/2 c. heavy cream
1 lb. fettuccine or spaghetti
Freshly-grated Parmesan or
  Romano cheese

Heat olive oil in a heavy sauté pan. Gently flavor oil with skinned garlic cloves. Remove cloves. Sauté floured chicken breasts. Cook through, remove from the pan and keep warm. Deglaze the pan with Marsala wine. Add the mushrooms and cook them, covered, as you reduce the wine by roughly one-half. Add heavy cream to the reduction and simmer until it becomes smooth and uniform. Cook noodles until al dente. Reserve 1/2 of the sauce. Add noodles to the remaining sauce in the sauté pan and toss. Top fettuccine with sliced chicken breast, remaining sauce and freshly-grated cheese.

"The great question...which I have not been able to answer...is.
What...does a women want?"

--Freud.
(Men, they are sooo - dumb!
Even a famous psychologist couldn't figure us out.) BJ

♟ Southwestern Shepherd's Pie

8 to 10 servings

This is great to fix when you have leftover mashed potatoes.

3 T. olive oil
2 T. unsalted butter
1 red onion, diced
2 ribs celery, diced
1 red bell pepper, cored, seeded & diced
1 green bell pepper, cored, seeded & diced
3 garlic cloves, minced
1 jalapeño, seeded & minced (I cut up slices from jar)
1/4 c. all-purpose flour
8 c. shredded cooked chicken, or cooked beef or lamb
1 c. dry white wine ☺

3 c. chicken broth, preferably homemade
1/4 c. chopped fresh parsley
2 tsp. chopped fresh thyme, or 1/2 heaping tsp. dried thyme
1 tsp. red pepper flakes
Kernels from 2 ears fresh corn (1 c. fresh or frozen corn)
Salt & freshly-ground black pepper, to taste
2 c. mashed potatoes made with milk
2 tsp. chili powder
Fresh parsley & fresh thyme, to garnish (opt.)

Preheat oven to 400°. Heat the olive oil and butter in large skillet over medium heat. Add the onion and cook, stirring frequently, until slightly brown, about 5 minutes. Add the celery, red bell pepper and green bell pepper, and cook 3 minutes more, stirring occasionally. Add the garlic and

Continued on following page.

Continued from preceding page.

jalapeño; cook 3 minutes more, stirring occasionally. Add the flour and cook, stirring constantly, until the flour starts to brown slightly, about 5 minutes. Add the chicken and wine; stir until the wine begins to evaporate, about 1 minute. Slowly add the chicken broth and continue to cook, stirring frequently, until the mixture begins to thicken and coats the back of a spoon. Reduce heat to low, bring the mixture to a low boil and cook 5 to 10 minutes, or until the mixture thickens and is creamy.

Remove from the heat and add the parsley, thyme, red pepper flakes and corn. Season with salt and pepper, and transfer the mixture to a 9x13-inch baking dish.

To make the chili mashed potatoes, mix mashed potatoes with 1 teaspoon of the chili powder in a bowl until well combined. Spoon the chili mashed potatoes on top of the chicken and bake 20 to 30 minutes, or until the potato peaks are slightly brown, and the chicken mixture is bubbling around the sides of the dish. Remove from the oven; sprinkle with the remaining chili powder, and the parsley and thyme if desired. Serve immediately.

"You can get by on charm for about 15 minutes.
After that, you better know something."
--H. Jackson Brown, Jr.
(Unless, of course, he is really good looking!) BJ

116

🍷 Cornish Hens with Apricot, Port and Balsamic Sauce

4 servings

Very good!

2 Cornish game hens, washed, patted dry & split down the center

Freshly-ground black pepper, to taste
8 slices bacon

SAUCE:
4 c. homemade chicken stock or canned reduced-sodium chicken broth
1/2 c. port wine ☺
1 c. dry red wine ☺

3/4 c. dried apricots, finely-chopped
1 T. balsamic vinegar
Salt & freshly-ground black pepper, to taste

Preheat oven to 400°. Place the hen halves in an ovenproof baking pan, skin-side up. Sprinkle them with pepper, and cover them with the bacon slices. Bake for 15 minutes, then reduce the oven temperature to 350° and bake for 20 to 25 minutes, or until the skin is crisp. Remove the birds from the oven and discard the bacon.

Sauce: In a medium saucepan, bring the stock or broth, to a boil over medium heat. Then reduce the heat to a simmer and cook for 10 to 15 minutes, or until the liquid is reduced to about 1 cup.

In another saucepan, combine the port and red wine. Bring the liquid to a boil. Reduce the heat to medium and cook for 10 minutes, or until the volume is reduced to about 1/2 cup. Pour the reduced stock, or broth, into the reduced wine. Stir in the apricots and vinegar. Cook for 10 minutes, or until the sauce is reduced by 1/3 and is thickened. Season with salt and pepper.

To serve, place a Cornish hen half in the center of each serving plate and spoon the sauce over the top. Serve this with mashed sweet potatoes, vegetable and salad.

Rock Cornish Hens with Burgundy Wine

4 servings

1 tsp. salt
1/4 tsp. ground cloves
1/4 tsp. ground nutmeg
1/4 tsp. freshly-ground pepper
1/4 tsp. ground thyme
4 Rock Cornish hens (about 1 lb. each)
4 slices bacon, halved

1 1/2 c. red Burgundy or other dry red wine ☺
1/2 tsp. instant chicken bouillon
1/2 c. boiling water
3 T. finely-chopped onion
3 T. chopped fresh parsley
4 c. cooked brown or white rice
1/2 c. currant jelly

Preheat oven to 350°. Mix salt, cloves, nutmeg, pepper and thyme; rub on skins and in cavities of hens. Place hens, breast-side up, on rack in shallow baking dish. Crisscross bacon slices over hens. Mix Burgundy, bouillon, water, onion and parsley; pour into baking dish.

Roast, uncovered, for 1 hour. Increase oven temperature to 400°. Roast until drumstick meat feels very soft when pressed, about 10 minutes. Transfer hens to warm serving platter. Remove bacon, dice and stir into rice. Strain hot juices from baking dish into a saucepan and skim off fat. Stir in currant jelly and heat, stirring constantly, until jelly is melted.

Arrange rice around hens on platter; spoon some sauce over hens. Garnish with sprigs of watercress. Pass remaining sauce.

♟ Sherried Turkey with Grapes

4 servings

2 c. med. cream sauce*
1/4 c. sherry ☺
1/4 lb. mushrooms, sliced
    lengthwise & sautéed in 2 T.
    butter (can use canned)

2 c. diced cooked turkey, cut in
    large pieces
1/2 c. green grapes, halved &
    seeded
1/2 c. red grapes, halved & seeded

Add sherry to cream sauce. Add mushrooms and turkey and heat. Just before serving, add grapes. Serve on reheated turkey stuffing, if you have some, on rice, or in puff pastry shells.

Pineapple may be used instead of grapes. You can add toasted, salted almonds at serving time.

*Forgot how to make cream sauce? Melt 4 tablespoons butter, 4 tablespoons flour, 1/2 teaspoon salt and a little pepper. Stir well and add gradually 2 cups milk. Stir until smooth and thickened.

"Adam and Eve had an ideal marriage. He didn't have to hear about all the men she could have married, and she didn't have to hear about the way his mother cooked."
--Kimberly Broyles

🍷 Turkey Scalloppini with Capers and Lemon

20 servings

For a big crowd.

20 (6 oz.) turkey breast medallions, pounded thin
2 c. flour
2 c. fresh breadcrumbs
Salt & pepper, to taste
Olive oil, as needed
2 T. shallots, chopped

1 T. minced garlic
1/2 c. capers, drained
1 c. dry white wine ☺
1 c. turkey or chicken stock
1 lb. butter, cubed & kept cold
2/3 c. fresh lemon juice
Lemon slices, for garnish

Pound turkey breasts into scaloppini filets. Mix flour and breadcrumbs with salt and pepper to taste.

Heat sauté pan with olive oil. Dredge turkey through the flour/breadcrumb mixture, then sauté both sides until fully cooked. Place onto a sheet pan and keep warm. Add shallots, garlic and capers to sauté pan and sauté until lightly golden. Deglaze pan with wine. Reduce by half. Add stock and reduce by half. Add butter and swirl in pan until all is melted into the sauce. Finish with lemon juice, salt and pepper to taste. Remove from heat.

"Wine is a constant proof that God loves us and loves to see us happy."
                                   --Benjamin Franklin
(I like this guy!) BJ

Baked Turkey Sandwiches

4 servings

1/4 c. butter
1/4 c. flour
1 2/3 c. milk
1/3 c. sherry ☺
1 (4 oz.) can mushroom stems & pieces, drained
Dash of mace

Salt & pepper
8 slices crisp toast, crusts removed
4 servings sliced, cooked turkey
8 slices crisp-cooked bacon, or ham slice
1/2 c. grated Cheddar cheese
Paprika

Melt butter and stir in flour. Add milk and cook, stirring constantly, until mixture boils and thickens. Add sherry, mushrooms, mace, salt and pepper. Place 2 slices toast, side by side, in each of 4 shallow individual baking dishes. Spread toast with some of the mushroom sauce; top with sliced turkey, then with bacon strips. Pour remaining sauce over all. Sprinkle with grated cheese and paprika. Bake 10 minutes, or until bubbly at 450°.

You have it easily in your power to increase the sum total of this world's happiness now. How? By giving a few words of sincere appreciation to someone who is lonely or discouraged. Perhaps you will forget tomorrow the kind words you say today, but the recipient may cherish them over a lifetime.
--Dale Carnegie

121

⟨ Turkey Timbales with Mushroom Wine Sauce

6 servings

6 T. butter or margarine
6 T. flour
1 1/2 c. milk or cream
1 c. turkey stock or chicken broth
1/2 c. white wine ☺
2 c. ground cooked turkey

1 1/2 c. soft breadcrumbs
2 eggs, slightly beaten
Salt & pepper, to taste
3 T. minced parsley
1 (2 oz.) can mushroom pieces

Melt butter and stir in flour; add milk, stock and wine. Cook, stirring constantly, until mixture is thickened and smooth. To 1 cup of this sauce, add the turkey, breadcrumbs, eggs, salt and pepper; blend well. Spoon mixture into 6 well-greased custard cups. Place in a shallow pan of hot water and bake in a moderate oven, 350°, for 30 minutes, or until firm. Add parsley and mushrooms (including the liquid) to remaining sauce. Season to taste with salt and pepper. Heat over boiling water. Unmold baked timbales and serve with the mushroom sauce.

"The best time to give advice to your children is while they're still young enough to believe you know what you're talking about."
--Unknown
(I hate it when they grow taller and smarter!) BJ

 Bourbon Chicken or Turkey

8 servings

1 turkey, or 2 (5 lb.) chickens, cut up

MARINADE:

1 c. dry red wine ☺
1/2 c. bourbon ☺
1/2 c. dry sherry ☺
1/3 c. soy sauce
3 T. vegetable oil

2 T. sugar
5 whole star anise
1 T. minced fresh ginger
Freshly-ground black pepper, to taste

GLAZE:

1 1/2 c. bourbon ☺
2/3 c. honey

2/3 c. ketchup
1/4 c. packed brown sugar

Have the turkey cut up as follows: drumsticks removed and cut crosswise through the bone, thighs removed and halved through the bone, breast removed (left on the bone) and each half cut into 4 or 5 pieces, and wings cut at elbows, tips discarded. Reserve the backs for another use. Rinse the pieces well and pat dry. Or buy 2 packages of pick of the chick.

Stir all the marinade ingredients together in a large bowl. Add the turkey pieces and coat them in the mixture. Cover and marinate for 1 hour.

Preheat oven to 325°. Lift the turkey or chicken pieces from the marinade, and arrange them in one or two roasting pans. Pour 1/2 cup of the marinade (or 1 cup if using 2 pans) over the turkey or chicken. Bake for 1 hour, turning and basting the pieces every 20 minutes. (If you are using two pans, rotate them after 30 minutes.) Increase the oven temperature to 450°.

Stir the glaze ingredients together in a bowl. Brush the turkey or chicken well with the glaze and bake 30 minutes, brushing and turning every 5 minutes. (If you are using two pans, rotate them after 15 minutes.) Mound the turkey or chicken on a large platter and serve.

Note: This is great hot or at room temperature.

Notes & Recipes

Meats
Beef - Pork - Lamb

FAVORITE RECIPES
FROM MY COOKBOOK

Recipe Name	Page Number

🍷 Châteaubriand

4 servings

2 to 3 lb. tenderloin of beef
Salt & freshly-ground pepper
1/2 lb. fresh mushrooms, sliced
3 T. butter
1 T. chopped chives
1 T. chopped fresh parsley

2 sm. shallots, chopped
1/2 tsp. salt
Dash of pepper
1 tsp. Worcestershire sauce
1/2 to 3/4 c. dry sherry ☺
2 T. brandy ☺

Salt and pepper meat as desired. Grill to desired doneness. Melt butter in a skillet over medium-high heat and sauté sliced mushrooms. Add chives, parsley and shallots; simmer for 5 minutes. Add seasonings and Worcestershire sauce; stir to combine. Blend in sherry and simmer. Add brandy just before serving and thin sauce with more sherry if desired. Spoon sauce over grilled meat.

🍷 Brainless Beef Sherry

5 lb. stew meat
1 pkg. dry onion soup mix
1 1/4 c. sherry ☺

3 cans cream of mushroom soup
1 c. water

Place all ingredients in roaster or other large pan suitable for oven. Cover and bake at 350° for 3 hours. You do not need to stir during cooking time.
Great for a crowd. Quick and easy.

125

Beef Filet with Peppercorns and Chutney

4 servings

Cracked black peppercorns, amount as desired (I use enough to cover both sides evenly)
4 (6 oz.) beef filet mignon, room temp.
5 T. butter, divided
8 oz. chutney
2 to 3 oz. cognac ☺

Press cracked peppercorns into filets with the heel of your hand. Heat 3 tablespoons butter in heavy skillet over high heat. Add filets just before butter begins to brown. Brown over high heat, approximately 3 minutes per side (for rare). Remove filets from skillet, reduce heat to low. Add remaining 2 tablespoons butter and chutney. Put cognac in a small saucepan and warm over low heat. Light cognac and carefully pour into chutney. After flames burn out, return filets to skillet and spoon sauce over them. Keep warm until serving.

"Childhood is that wonderful time when all you need to do to lose weight is take a bath."
--Richard Zera

Burgundy Pot Roast

8 or more servings

This unusually delicious beef makes wonderful hot or cold sandwiches later in the week. I have made this roast a million times and my family and guests cry for more gravy. The aroma will knock your socks off.

5 lb. beef rump, eye of round, or chuck, rolled & tied	1 1/2 c. Burgundy ☺
	1/2 c. finely-chopped onion
Flour	1/2 c. finely-chopped celery
Salt & pepper	1/4 c. finely-chopped parsley
2 T. drippings or oil	1/4 tsp. oregano
1 (8 oz.) can tomato sauce	1/4 tsp. sweet basil

Dredge meat with flour, seasoned with salt and pepper. Brown slowly on all sides in drippings. Add all remaining ingredients; season to taste with salt and pepper. Cover and simmer gently about 4 hours, or until beef is tender, turning meat occasionally. Transfer to hot platter. Measure liquid in kettle and add water, if necessary, to make 4 cups; heat to boiling. Blend 1/4 cup flour with 1/2 cup cold water to make a smooth paste; stir slowly into boiling liquid. Cook, stirring constantly, for 2 to 3 minutes. Taste and add salt and pepper, if necessary. Serve with meat.

Note: I make this on Sunday. Put it in the oven before church on low heat (250°) and cook all day.

🍷 Lobster-Stuffed Tenderloin of Beef

8 servings

Another to-die-for recipe!

3 to 4 lb. whole beef tenderloin
2 (4 oz.) lobster tails
1 T. butter or margarine, melted

1 1/2 tsp. lemon juice
6 slices bacon, partially cooked

BÉARNAISE SAUCE:
1 c. melted butter
4 egg yolks, room temp.
Juice of 1 med. lemon
1 1/2 tsp. Worcestershire sauce
Ground red pepper, to taste
4 T. dry white wine, divided ☺

1 T. finely-minced shallots
2 tsp. finely-crumbled dried
tarragon, or 2 T. chopped fresh
tarragon
Salt, to taste

GARNISH:
Fluted mushrooms, for garnish

Watercress, for garnish

Preheat oven to 425°. Cut beef tenderloin lengthwise to within 1/2-inch of bottom to butterfly. Place frozen lobster tails in boiling salted water to cover. Return to boiling. Reduce heat and simmer for 5 to 6 minutes. Carefully remove lobster from shells. Cut in halves lengthwise. Place lobster, end to end, inside beef. Combine the butter and lemon juice. Drizzle on lobster. Close meat around lobster. Tie roast together securely with kitchen string at 1-inch intervals. Place on rack in shallow roasting pan. Bake for 45 to 50 minutes for rare. Lay bacon slices on top. Roast 5 more minutes.

Continued on following page.

Continued from preceding page.

Béarnaise Sauce: Whisk egg yolks, lemon juice, Worcestershire sauce and red pepper in top of double boiler over simmering water until thick and a sheen forms, approximately 3 minutes, but not more than 5 minutes. Begin adding melted butter in a steady stream, whisking constantly until all has been added. Add 2 tablespoons of wine and whisk well. The sauce should be light and fluffy. In a small saucepan, heat the remaining wine, shallots and tarragon until liquid evaporates. Remove from heat and add to sauce, mixing well. Add salt to taste. Hold at room temperature until serving time.

Slice roast and arrange on platter. Spoon on Béarnaise Sauce and garnish with fluted whole mushrooms and watercress.

"Wine can of their wits the wise beguile,
Make the sage frolic, and the serious smile."
--Homer, "The Odyssey" (9th c. B.C.)

Beef Tenderloin in Mushroom Port Sauce

6 servings

1 T. olive oil
2 lg. cloves garlic, minced
1/2 tsp. salt
1/2 tsp. coarsely-ground black pepper
3 to 4 lb. well-trimmed beef tenderloin roast, center cut
3 T. butter
1 lb. mixed fresh mushrooms, stems removed & cut in half if large

1/4 c. finely-chopped shallots
1 1/4 c. good port wine ☺
1 (13 3/4 to 14 1/2 oz.) can ready-to-serve beef broth
1/3 c. coarse-grain Dijon-style mustard
1 T. cornstarch, dissolved in 2 T. water
1 T. butter, softened (opt.)

Heat oven to 425°. Combine olive oil, garlic, salt and pepper. Press evenly into surface of beef. Heat large nonstick skillet over medium-high heat until hot. Brown beef evenly on all sides to sear. Transfer to rack in shallow roasting pan. Insert meat thermometer so tip is centered in thickest part of roast, not resting in fat. Do not add water or cover. Roast in 425° oven about 30 to 35 minutes for medium-rare to medium doneness.

Meanwhile, in the same skillet, heat 1 1/2 tablespoons butter over medium-high heat until hot. Add 1/2 of mushrooms and the shallots. Cook and stir until mushrooms are tender. Remove from skillet. Repeat with remaining butter and mushrooms. Set aside.

In same skillet, bring port wine to a boil over high heat. Cook 5 to 7 minutes, or until almost syrupy (reduced to about 2 tablespoons). Stir in broth, mustard and cornstarch mixture. Cook until slightly thickened and bubbly, stirring occasionally. Return mushrooms to sauce.

Remove roast from oven when meat thermometer registers 135°. Transfer roast to carving board. Tent loosely with aluminum foil. Let stand 15 minutes. (Temperature will continue to rise about 10 degrees to reach 145° for medium rare.)

Carve roast into slices. If desired, immediately before serving, stir 1 tablespoon softened butter into sauce. Serve with roast.

🍷 Pan-Roasted Beef Tenderloin with Rosemary and Garlic

4 to 6 servings

1 (3 to 4 lb.) beef tenderloin roast
4 fresh rosemary sprigs
1 garlic clove, minced
Salt & freshly-ground pepper, to taste
1 T. vegetable oil

5 shallots, minced
2 c. dry red wine (like a good Cabernet) ☺
2 sticks softened unsalted butter, cut into 1/2" pieces

Preheat oven to 400°. Let the roast stand at room temperature for 30 to 40 minutes. Set the roast on a clean work surface and lay the rosemary sprigs lengthwise along the roast. Using kitchen twine, tie the rosemary to the roast at 2-inch intervals. Rub the roast with the garlic and season with salt and pepper.

Preheat an oval skillet or large sauté pan over medium-high heat and warm the vegetable oil. Add the roast and brown, 3 to 4 minutes per side. Transfer the skillet to the oven and roast, turning the beef occasionally, until an instant-read thermometer inserted into the center of the meat registers 125° for very rare to rare, 15 to 20 minutes, or until done to your liking. Transfer the roast to a cutting board, cover loosely with aluminum foil and let rest for 5 minutes.

Meanwhile, in a saucepan over medium-high heat, combine the shallots and wine and boil until reduced to 1/4 cup, 7 to 10 minutes. Add the butter, a few pieces at a time, whisking constantly until blended before adding more. Strain the sauce through a fine-mesh sieve and season with salt. Keep warm over very low heat, being careful not to boil.

Sautéed Filet Mignon

2 servings

2 (1 1/4" to 1 1/2" thick) filet
  mignon steaks (1 to1 1/2 lb.)

Salt & freshly-ground black
  pepper
1 tsp. chopped fresh rosemary

BALSAMIC VINEGAR PAN SAUCE:

2 tsp. minced garlic
1/3 c. dry vermouth ☺
1/4 c. beef or chicken stock
2 tsp. soy sauce

1 T. balsamic vinegar
1 T. butter (opt.)
Salt & freshly-ground black
  pepper

Season the filet mignon steaks generously with salt and pepper. Sprinkle with the rosemary. In a medium, heavy skillet, heat the oil over medium-high heat. Put in the filet mignon steaks, and fry them for 4 to 5 minutes per side for medium-rare (the internal temperature should be 120° to 130°). Remove and cover loosely to keep them warm while you prepare the sauce.

Balsamic Vinegar Pan Sauce: Pour off all but 1 tablespoon of the fat, leaving any meat juices in the pan. Reduce the heat to medium and sauté the garlic for 15 seconds, stirring. Add the vermouth and scrape up any browned bits from the bottom of the pan. Raise the heat to high and reduce the vermouth to a syrup. Pour in the stock, soy sauce and vinegar. Boil until the sauce just reduces to a syrup. Remove from the heat and stir in the butter, if you wish. (It adds fat but gives the sauce a velvety texture). Taste for salt and pepper. Pour over the filet mignon steaks and serve.

132

Beef in Herb Wine Sauce

4 to 6 servings

Serve this gourmet entrée over fluffy rice and with a green salad.

2 lb. lean sirloin tip, cut into 1 1/2"
  cubes
3 or 4 med. onions, sliced
2 T. oil
1 1/2 T. flour
1 c. beef bouillon
1 1/2 c. red wine ☺
1/4 tsp. marjoram

1/4 tsp. thyme
1/4 tsp. oregano
1 tsp. salt
1/2 tsp. pepper
1/2 lb. fresh mushrooms, sliced
  lengthwise, sautéed in 1/4 c.
  butter

Sauté onions in oil until yellow; remove from pan. Add meat cubes, sprinkle lightly with flour and brown meat. Add half the bouillon, half the wine and the herbs and seasonings. Cover pan tightly and simmer over low heat (or in a 350° oven) about 2 hours, gradually adding remaining bouillon and wine. Add onions and mushrooms; cook about 30 minutes longer, or until meat is tender.

*"I have yet to hear a man ask for advice on
how to combine marriage and a career."*
--Unknown

♏ Green Pepper Steak

4 servings

1 1/2 lb. round steak
Flour
Salt & pepper
1/4 c. oil
3 green peppers, cut in strips

2 onions, chopped
1 c. stock or broth
1/2 c. red wine* ☺
1 tsp. Worcestershire sauce

Cut the steak into serving-size pieces, flour and season, and brown on both sides in hot oil. Prepare vegetables, setting green peppers aside, and adding onions to meat, along with 1 cup stock. Cover and simmer gently until meat is tender, 1 hour. Add peppers, wine and Worcestershire sauce. Cover and cook gently 20 minutes longer. Remove meat and vegetables to hot platter and thicken drippings for gravy, if necessary.

Note: *White wine may be used in place of red wine, without impairing this good dish.

*"Some see the glass as half-empty, some the glass as half-full.
I see the glass as too big."*
--Lisa Leslie
(Except when it comes to a wine glass, the bigger the better!)

 Steak Diane

4 to 6 servings

4 to 6 (3 to 4 oz.) center-cut beef
   tenderloin medallions, trimmed
   of all fat & pounded to 1/2" thick,
   chilled
1 1/2 oz. clarified butter
1 tsp. Worcestershire sauce
2 T. shallots, chopped fine
1/8 tsp. garlic, minced
1/4 c. mushroom caps, sliced 1/8"
   thick
1 T. lemon juice, fresh squeezed

1 tsp. dry mustard powder
1/2 tsp. thyme leaves, fresh if
   possible
2 oz. heavy cream
4 tsp. brandy ☺
1 T. parsley, chopped
1 T. chives, chopped
Salt (about 1/2 tsp., or to taste)
Fresh ground black pepper (1/8
   tsp., or to taste)

In a small 8- to 10-inch sauté pan, heat 1 tablespoon butter over medium
heat for 1 minute. Add the tenderloin steaks, sprinkle with a little salt and
pepper. Increase heat to medium-high and sauté exactly 2 minutes on each
side. Remove them to a plate and chill in a refrigerator for 5 minutes.

Preheat a large (12-inch) sauté pan over medium heat for 1 minute. Add
clarified butter, then add the Worcestershire sauce to the butter. Place the
shallots, garlic and mushrooms in the center of the pan with the tenderloin
steaks around the edges. With a spoon, stir and toss the mushroom
mixture. After 2 minutes, add the lemon juice and season the ingredients
with salt and fresh ground black pepper. Turn the filet mignon steaks and
add the thyme, chopped parsley and dried mustard powder. Cook the
steaks to the doneness you like. Leave them in the pan and add the heavy
cream and chives. Tilt the pan slightly, and pour the brandy into the front
edge of the pan; turn the heat to high and let the flame (or if electric, light

Continued on following page.

Continued from preceding page.

with a match) catch the brandy's vapors and ignite it. Swirl slightly, turn off the heat and let the flame go out.

Place filet mignon medallions on plates and top with the sauce from the pan.

Note: I slightly undercook the filet mignon steaks prior to adding the cream and brandy so that the reduction process of making the sauce doesn't overcook them.

♉ Boeuf Bourguignon

10 servings

5 lb. boneless beef, cut in large cubes	2 T. brandy ☺
1 1/2 lb. (about 10 med.) onions, diced	1 1/2 to 2 c. red table wine ☺
	Parsley
2 carrots, diced	Thyme
1/3 c. butter	Bay leaves
6 slices bacon, cut crosswise in strips	Salt
	Pepper
1/2 c. flour	1 lb. mushrooms, sliced & browned in 1/4 c. butter

Brown onions and carrots in butter; remove from pan and add beef and bacon. Brown meat cubes. Stir in flour. Pour brandy over meat and set aflame. Add vegetables, wine, herbs, salt and pepper; cover. Simmer 45 minutes. Remove meat from sauce; put sauce through strainer or food mill and return to pan with meat. Add mushrooms and simmer for 2 hours, covered. Serve with rice, noodles or homemade croutons.

136

Steaks with Red Wine Sauce

4 servings

2 (12 oz.) boneless beef top loin steaks, 3/4" thick, well trimmed	1 garlic clove, minced
1/4 tsp. salt	2 T. tomato paste
1 T. olive oil	3/4 c. dry red wine ☺
1 med. onion, finely chopped	1/2 c. chicken broth
	1/2 tsp. Worcestershire sauce

Heat nonstick 12-inch skillet over medium-high heat until very hot, but not smoking. Add steaks; sprinkle with salt. Cook 8 to 10 minutes for medium-rare, or until done, turning steaks over once. Transfer steaks to plate. Cut each steak crosswise in half; cover with foil to keep warm.

In same skillet, in oil, cook onion over medium heat, 8 minutes, or until tender, stirring occasionally. Add garlic and cook 1 minute, stirring. Stir in tomato paste and wine and heat to boiling; boil 1 minute. Add broth and Worcestershire sauce; heat through.

Pour any juice from the steak plate into sauce in skillet; spoon sauce over steaks.

"You know your children have grown up when they stop asking you where they came from and refuse to tell you where they are going."
--Unknown

137

🍷 Steak au Poivre

2 servings

Bourbon or red wine may be substituted for the cognac. You can put on a show with this one. One of my favorites. Don't drink unless someone else lights the fire.

1 thick-cut well-marbled strip steak, about 1 lb. total weight & 1/2" thick	Salt
	1 tsp. vegetable oil
	1 T. butter
2 T. mixed whole peppercorns, including black, white & green pepper	

PAN SAUCE:

2 T. minced shallots	1 T. unsalted butter, at room temp.
3 T. cognac (or bourbon or red wine) ☺	Chopped parsley, for garnish
	Watercress, for garnish
1/2 c. flavorful dark stock	

Trim the steak of all the surrounding fat and cartilage. Cut the meat into 2 pieces and crush the peppercorns using the bottom of a heavy skillet or rolling pin. Sprinkle salt to taste on the top and bottom of the steaks, then press each side into the cracked peppercorns, encrusting the steaks lightly or heavily, as you like.

Continued on following page.

Continued from preceding page.

Heat the oil and the butter in a heavy sauté or frying pan over high heat. When the pan is very hot, lay the peppered steaks in. Fry for about 1 1/2 to 2 minutes, until the undersides are well seared. Turn the meat and cook the second side for about a minute. Press with a finger to test for the slight springiness that indicates rare. Cook to desired doneness and remove to a warm platter

Pan Sauce: Add the shallots to the pan and sauté briefly, stirring with a spoon to scrape up the drippings. Lean away from the stove (averting your face) and pour the cognac into the pan; tilt the edge of the pan slightly, over the burner flame, to ignite the alcohol. The cognac will flame for a few seconds as the alcohol burns off. Cook for a few moments more and then add the stock. Bring the liquid back to the boil, and cook about 1 minute to thicken the sauce, stirring occasionally. Taste and adjust seasoning. Finally, add the soft butter, swirling the pan until it melts and incorporates with the juices.

When blended, pour the sauce over the steaks. Sprinkle liberally with chopped parsley and garnish each plate with sprigs of parsley or watercress.

"Whatever women do they must do twice as well as men to be thought half as good. Luckily, this is not difficult."

--Charlotte Whittond

Brisket Braised in White Wine

4 to 6 servings

1 T. oil
3 lb. beef brisket
Salt & freshly-ground pepper, to
  taste
2/3 c. dry white wine ☺
1 med. onion, diced
4 garlic cloves, minced
2 med. tomatoes, coarsely chopped
4 carrots, peeled

4 med. parsnips, peeled
1/2 c. chicken stock, or more
1/4 c. water
1 tsp. dried thyme
1 tsp. dried rosemary
1 bay leaf
12 juniper berries, crushed*
  (smash with meat porender or
  skillet)

Heat oven to 225°. Heat oil in large Dutch oven over medium-high heat. Season brisket with salt and pepper and then sear (cook over high heat to brown the exterior) on both sides in pan. Remove brisket, turn heat to high and add white wine. With a wooden spoon, scrape bottom of pan and reduce wine for 1 minute. Add onion and cook over medium heat for 5 minutes. Add garlic and cook for 1 minute. Return brisket to pan with tomatoes, carrots, parsnips, chicken stock, water, thyme, rosemary, bay leaf and juniper berries. Bring to a simmer. Cover, place in oven and bake for about 2 1/2 to 3 hours, or until meat is tender (about 145° internal temperature). Discard bay leaf.

Remove brisket and slice against the grain into thin slices. Arrange on plates with carrots and parsnips, adding broth to each serving.

Note: *Juniper berries are the deep purple fruit from a Juniper bush. They have a bittersweet, pine flavor with a peppery aftertaste. Great with beef, game, pork, venison and cabbage. Can order on the internet if you can't find them.

Beef Short Ribs Braised with Citrus

4 to 6 servings

4 lb. bone-in short ribs, trimmed
  of exterior fat
Salt & freshly-ground black
  pepper
4 T. olive oil (divided use)
4 oranges (divided use)
4 lemons (divided use)
4 limes (divided use)
1 lg. onion, peeled & roughly
  chopped
1 lg. carrot, peeled & roughly
  chopped

1 stalk celery, roughly chopped
1 T. whole coriander seeds
5 lg. garlic cloves, peeled &
  smashed
1 btl. fruity white wine (like
  Vouvray) ☺
3 branches fresh thyme
4 stems parsley
1 bay leaf
1 sm. head white cabbage (opt.)
1/4 c. chopped cilantro, for garnish

Season ribs with salt and pepper. Heat 2 tablespoons oil on high heat in a deep, heavy casserole. Brown the ribs well on all sides; this will take about 20 minutes. Remove ribs, pour out fat and wipe out the pan.

Meanwhile, use a vegetable peeler to remove the zest (colored part only of the rind), then squeeze the juice from 2 oranges, 2 lemons and 2 limes. Preheat oven to 350°.

Put remaining 2 tablespoons of oil in pan, turn heat to medium-high and add the zests, onion, carrot, celery, coriander, garlic and a large pinch of salt and pepper to taste. Cook, stirring until the onions are soft, about 10

Continued on following page.

141

Continued from preceding page.

minutes. Add white wine, orange, lemon and lime juices, thyme, parsley and bay leaf to the pan and bring to a boil; add the ribs, cover and put in the oven. Cook until the meat is very tender and falling from the bone, about 3 hours; turn the meat once or twice during cooking.

While ribs are cooking, core and quarter the cabbage. Separate the leaves and boil in salted water until tender, about 5 minutes (you may microwave the cabbage with 1/3 cup water, covered, for about 3 minutes). Drain, then rinse with cold water to stop the cooking. Set aside.

Remove zest from the remaining fruit and save. Cut each fruit in half and section as you would a grapefruit, removing any seeds; do this over a bowl so you catch all the juices.

Transfer ribs to a platter. Strain the vegetables and liquid into another pan, pressing hard on the vegetables to extract all of their juices. (At this point, all the dish's components may be refrigerated.) Bring strained juice to a boil. If a thicker sauce is desired, whisk in 1 tablespoon butter and cook until slightly thickened. Add the ribs, citrus sections and cabbage. Heat the ribs through, adjust the seasoning as necessary, and serve, garnished with citrus zest and cilantro.

A very different flavor! Excellent!

Easy Wine - Marinated Brisket

8 servings

1 1/2 c. dry red or white wine ☺
2 T. soy sauce
1 sm. onion, grated
1 celery stalk, thinly sliced
3 garlic cloves, finely minced
3 to 4 lb. beef brisket
1 med.-sized onion, thinly sliced

Preheat oven to 325°. Combine wine, soy sauce, grated onion, celery and garlic in a large heavy-duty zip-top freezer bag large enough to accommodate the brisket. Add the brisket to the bag, squeeze out the air, seal, and refrigerate 3 to 4 hours, turning occasionally.

Remove brisket and place fat-side up in a roasting pan or Dutch oven. Spread sliced onions around brisket and cover with half the marinade. Reserve remaining marinade. Cover tightly with heavy foil or a lid. Bake 3 hours, until tender. Check midway during roasting time and add more marinade, if needed, to keep brisket from drying out. (Discard any remaining marinade when brisket is done.)

When done, remove brisket from oven and let rest 15 minutes. Carve slices against the grain and place on serving platter. Cover slices with pan juices and cooked onions to serve.

Stringed Beef Brisket

4 to 6 servings

Kosher salt, to taste
Freshly-ground black pepper, to
  taste
1 (6 lb.) beef brisket, cut in 1/2"
  cubes
3/4 c. peanut oil
1 carrot, peeled & chopped
1 leek, washed & diced

1 stalk celery, diced
2 T. puréed garlic
1 onion, chopped
2 c. Cabernet Sauvignon wine ☺
12 c. veal or beef stock
1 bay leaf
2 T. dried thyme
1/2 c. cognac ☺

Salt and pepper the brisket. Brown meat in half the hot oil in a sauté pan. Remove and set aside. Brown carrot, leek, celery, garlic and onion in the remaining oil in the same pan. Remove and deglaze with 1/3 cup Cabernet.

Place brisket, vegetables and deglazed juices in a stockpot. Add the Cabernet Sauvignon, veal stock, bay leaf, thyme, and all except 2 tablespoons of the cognac. Add salt and pepper to taste. Cover and cook until meat is tender (about 2 hours). Remove the meat, and using 2 forks, shred the beef.

Meanwhile, reduce sauce over low heat, uncovered, until thick enough to coat a spoon. Adjust seasonings and return brisket to the sauce. Add the remaining 2 tablespoons cognac and serve the meat mounded up on a platter.

Slow Cooker Burgundy Meat Loaf

6 servings

2 lb. ground beef or mixture of
   beef, pork & veal
1 med. onion, chopped
2 eggs
1 c. soft white breadcrumbs
1/2 c. parsley, chopped
1/2 c. dry red Burgundy wine ☺

1 T. fresh basil
1 1/2 tsp. salt
1/2 tsp. pepper
5 slices bacon
1 bay leaf
8 oz. tomato sauce with
   mushrooms, heated

Combine ground meat, onion, eggs, breadcrumbs, parsley, Burgundy, basil, salt and pepper in a large bowl; mix. Crisscross 3 bacon slices on a 12-inch square of aluminum foil; shape meat loaf mixture into a 6-inch round on top of bacon. Top with remaining bacon slices, halved, and bay leaf. Lift foil with loaf into slow cooker; cover. Cook on high 1 hour; turn heat control to low; cook 4 hours longer, or until meat loaf is well done. Remove loaf from slow cooker by lifting the foil, tilting fat back into the slow cooker. Discard bacon and bay leaf.

Note: Serve on heated platter and spoon part of the heated tomato sauce over.

Serving Suggestion: Serve with buttered noodles and French green beans.

Beef Brisket with Carmelized Onions and Wine Sauce

8 servings

A unique taste with caramelized onions and dried cherries. Very good.

1 (4 to 5 lb.) flat-cut brisket
Salt & freshly-ground pepper, to
    taste
2 T. olive oil
1 1/2 c. chopped yellow onion
1/2 c. diced carrot

2 garlic cloves, finely chopped
1 (28 oz.) can plum tomatoes, with
    juices
2 1/2 c. Merlot or other full-bodied
    red wine (Cabernet) ☺
1 bay leaf

CARAMELIZED ONIONS:
2 T. olive oil
3 c. thinly-sliced sweet onions,
    such as Vidalia

Salt & freshly-ground pepper, to
    taste
1/2 c. pitted dried cherries

Preheat oven to 325°. Season the brisket on all sides with salt and pepper. In a Dutch oven or a large, wide ovenproof pan with a tight-fitting lid, warm the olive oil over medium-high heat. Add the brisket and brown well on both sides, about 6 minutes total. Transfer to a plate. Add the onion and carrot to the pan and sauté until golden, about 5 minutes. Add the garlic and sauté until softened, about 1 minute. Add the tomatoes and juices, 1 cup of the Merlot and the bay leaf. Mix well and bring to a boil. Return the brisket to the pan, cover and place in the oven.

Continued on following page.

Continued from preceding page.

Cook, basting occasionally with the pan juices, until the brisket is fork tender, about 3 hours. Remove from the oven and let cool in the juices. Carefully lift the brisket from the juices and transfer it to a deep platter. Cover with aluminum foil and refrigerate until cold, at least 2 hours or up to overnight. Let the pan juices cool, then pass through a food mill or press through a sieve into a bowl. Discard the solids and refrigerate the juices until ready to use.

Just before serving, preheat the oven to 350°. Cut the brisket across the grain into thin slices. Arrange the slices, slightly overlapping, on an ovenproof serving platter. Cover with aluminum foil and place in the oven for 15 minutes to heat through.

Meanwhile, cook the onions. In a large frypan over medium-low heat, warm the olive oil. Add the onions and sauté, stirring often, until golden brown, about 20 minutes. Season with salt and pepper. While the onions are cooking, pour the remaining 1 1/2 cups Merlot into a saucepan over high heat. Add 1/4 cup of the dried cherries and cook until reduced by half, about 5 minutes. Stir in the puréed brisket juices and heat some more. Season with salt and pepper.

To serve, remove the brisket from the oven. Pour the sauce evenly over the top. Top with the caramelized onions and the remaining 1/4 cup dried cherries. Serve immediately.

Marinated Hamburgers

4 to 8 burgers

1 to 2 lb. ground beef chuck
1 tsp. salt
1/2 tsp. pepper
1/2 c. soy sauce
1/2 c. sherry ☺
1/2 tsp. ginger
4 split, toasted buns

Mix meat, salt and pepper and shape into 4 patties. Marinate for an hour in mixture of soy sauce, sherry and ginger. Drain and cook burgers on grill of outdoor fire or broil them.

Potatoed Pork Loin

2 servings

2 T. oil
1 med. Idaho potato, julienned
Salt & freshly-ground pepper
2 T. butter
5 (2 oz.) pork loin slices
3 T. Marsala wine ☺

Potatoes: Heat oil in sauté pan over high heat. Let pan become very hot. Toss potato sticks into pan. Season with salt and pepper. Allow potatoes to cook until they form one large crust. Flip over to cook other side. They are finished on each side when they break free from the pan when shaken. Remove from pan and keep warm.

Melt butter in same pan. Season pork with salt and pepper; place in pan. Sauté until done, about 2 minutes. Remove pork from pan and place over potato crust. Deglaze pan with Marsala wine. Pour over pork to serve.

♈ Pork Tenderloin in Dijon Sauce

4 T. butter, divided
1 T. vegetable oil
1 1/2 lb. pork tenderloin, cut in 1"
  slices
1 onion, chopped
1 1/4 c. dry white wine ☺

1/3 c. cider vinegar
10 peppercorns, crushed
Salt
1 1/2 c. whipping cream
2 T. Dijon mustard

Sauté tenderloin slices in 2 tablespoons butter and oil in large heavy skillet over medium heat. Brown pork for 1 minute on each side. Add onion and sauté until translucent. Add wine, bring to a boil, reduce heat to lowest setting, partially cover and let gently simmer for about 30 minutes, or until meat is cooked through. Transfer meat to platter and keep warm.

Add vinegar to pan along with peppercorns. Let cook until sauce is reduced to no more than 2/3 cup. Add salt to taste and cream; simmer for about 5 minutes. Stir in Dijon mustard, simmer for several minutes longer and swirl in butter. Spoon sauce over medallions and serve with rice.

"I'm strong, I'm tough, I still wear my eyeliner."
--Lisa Leslie

♀ Roast Pork with Apricot Demi-Glace

Serves 8 to 10

This tender pork roast makes a delicious main course. For a large holiday gathering, serve it alongside a turkey, prime rib or other roast.

1 (6 lb.) boneless pork loin, tied with kitchen twine
Salt & freshly-ground pepper, to taste
6 T. (3/4 stick) unsalted butter
1 1/2 c. light red wine, such as Pinot Noir ☺
Bouquet garni (1 bay leaf, 6 to 8 fresh thyme sprigs & 2 fresh sage leaves, tied together with kitchen twine; put in cheese cloth so you can remove it)

1/4 c. veal demi-glace mixed with 1 cup warmed chicken stock
1/3 c. port ☺
1/3 c. apricot jam
1/4 c. slivered dried apricots, soaked in hot water for 20 minutes
Pomegranate seeds, for garnish
Minced fresh flat-leaf parsley, for garnish

Position a rack in the lower third of oven and preheat to 350°. Let the pork stand at room temperature for about 1 hour. Season with salt and pepper. In a roasting pan over medium-high heat, melt 3 tablespoons of the butter. When hot, add the pork and brown, 4 to 5 minutes per side. Add the wine and bouquet garni. Transfer the pan to the oven and roast, basting occasionally with the pan juices, until an instant-read thermometer inserted into the center of the meat registers 140° for medium, about 1 1/2 hours; 150° for medium-well, about 1 3/4 hours; or until done to your liking. Transfer the pork to a carving board, cover loosely with aluminum foil and let rest for about 10 minutes before carving.

Continued on following page.

Continued from preceding page.

Set the roasting pan over medium-high heat and add the demi-glace mixture and port, stirring to scrape up any browned bits. Stir in the apricot jam and dried apricots. Increase the heat to high and cook, stirring, until the sauce is thick enough to coat a spoon, 8 to 10 minutes. Carve the pork into slices 1/2-inch thick and arrange on a warmed platter. Stir the remaining 3 tablespoons butter into the sauce and season with salt and pepper. Return to a boil and cook for 1 to 2 minutes more. Pour the sauce over the pork, garnish with pomegranate seeds and parsley, and serve immediately.

♟ Barbecued Pork Tenderloin

4 servings

Sherry, soy sauce and honey give this unusual barbecue sauce a celestial flavor.

2 (1 1/2 lb.) pork tenderloins	**3 T. honey**
2 T. soy sauce	**1/4 tsp. powdered ginger**
3 T. sherry ☺	**1 tsp. salt**

Place tenderloins in a large bowl. Combine remaining ingredients and pour over meat. Cover and chill several hours, or overnight. Bake in a covered casserole at 350° for 2 hours. Remove cover last 30 minutes. Baste with sauce a few times during baking. Cut into thin slices.

Spareribs, Apples and Sauerkraut

4 servings

5 lb. meaty spareribs	2 onions, sliced
3 T. butter	1 carrot, grated
1 dash of pepper	3 apples, sliced
1 qt. sauerkraut, rinsed	1 2/3 to 2 c. dry white wine ☺

Preheat oven to 350°. In skillet, lightly brown spareribs in butter. Sprinkle with pepper. In separate bowl, mix together sauerkraut, onions and carrots. Place half this mixture in baking dish. Add half the apple slices and all the spareribs. Cover with remaining sauerkraut mixture, apple slices and wine. Cover and bake 1 hour and 45 minutes.

"I'm out of estrogen, and I have a gun."
--Unknown

Rum Roasted Pork

Serves 8

2 garlic cloves, crushed
3 T. soy sauce
1 T. malt vinegar
1 T. finely-chopped celery
1/2 T. chopped spring onion
  (scallion)
1 1/2 tsp. dried thyme
1 tsp. dried sage
1/2 tsp. ground mixed spice
  (pumpkin pie spice)

1/2 tsp. curry powder
1/2 c. (4 oz.) rum ☺
1 T. (raw) sugar
3 1/2 lb. boned loin of pork
Salt & ground black pepper
Spring onion (scallion) curls, to
  garnish
Creamed sweet potato, to serve

SAUCE:
2 T. butter or margarine, diced
1 T. tomato purée (paste)
1 1/4 c. chicken or pork stock

1 T. chopped fresh parsley
1 T. (raw) sugar
Hot pepper sauce, to taste

   In a bowl, mix the garlic, soy sauce, vinegar, celery, spring onion, thyme, sage, spice, curry powder, rum and sugar. Add a little salt and pepper.
   Open out the pork and slash the meat, without cutting through it completely. Place it in a shallow dish. Spread most of the spice mixture all over the pork, pressing it well into the slashes. Rub the outside of the joint with the remaining mixture, cover the dish with clear film (plastic wrap) and chill in the refrigerator overnight.

Continued on following page.

Continued from preceding page.

Preheat the oven to 350°. Roll the meat up, then tie it tightly in several places with strong cotton string to hold the meat together. Spread a large piece of foil across a roasting pan and place the marinated pork loin in the center. Baste the pork with a few spoonfuls of the marinade and wrap the foil around the meat. Roast the pork in the oven for 1 1/2 hours, then slide the foil out from under the meat and discard it. Baste the pork with any remaining marinade and cook for approximately 1 hour. Check occasionally that the meat is not drying out and baste with the pan juices.

Meanwhile, make the sauce. Transfer the pork to a warmed serving dish, cover with foil and leave to stand in a warm place for 15 minutes. Pour the pan juices into a pan. Add the butter or margarine, tomato purée, stock, parsley and sugar, with hot pepper sauce and salt to taste. Simmer until reduced.

Serve the pork sliced, with the creamed sweet potato. Garnish with the spring onion curls and serve the sauce separately.

Make a day ahead.

♀ Teriyaki Pork Tenderloin

3/4 c. Kikkoman teriyaki marinade & sauce	2 T. brown sugar
1/3 c. bourbon ☺	2 garlic cloves, minced
	2 (1 3/4 to 2 lb.) pork tenderloins

Mix the marinade, bourbon, sugar and garlic thoroughly. Cover the tenderloins with the marinade. Put them in a plastic bag and chill for several hours, or overnight, turning the bag frequently to ensure that both tenderloins are covered in marinade.

The tenderloins taste the best on the grill. But you can also do it in the oven at 400° for about 20 minutes. Be sure to baste them to keep them moist.

154

Pork Tenderloins Braised with Red Cabbage

6 servings

3 pork tenderloins
1 1/2 c. Pinot Noir ☺
1/2 c. olive oil
1 T. balsamic vinegar
2 bay leaves, crumbled
2 cloves garlic, mashed
Ground cloves
2 T. olive oil
3 thick slices bacon
1 lg. red onion, thinly sliced

4 med. carrots, peeled, sliced or
   julienned
1 (2 lb.) red cabbage, cored &
   thinly shredded
1/2 c. beef stock (homemade or
   canned)
1 tsp. salt
1/8 tsp. freshly-ground black
   pepper
Steamed baby carrots, for garnish

Trim the tenderloins of all fat and silver skin. Combine the Pinot Noir, 1/2 cup olive oil, balsamic vinegar, bay leaves, garlic and a pinch of ground cloves in a noncorrosive bowl and whisk to mix well. Add the tenderloin and turn to coat well. Marinate, covered, at room temperature for 1 hour, or in the refrigerator for 8 hours or longer, turning 2 or 3 times.

Remove the tenderloins to drain on paper towels, reserving the marinade. Cut the tenderloins into halves. Brown in 2 tablespoons olive oil in a large, heavy sauté pan. Remove the pork.

Cut the bacon into 1/4-inch strips. Add to the sauté pan. Cook over low heat just until light brown. Add the onion and sliced or julienned carrots. Cook for 3 or 4 minutes, stirring occasionally. Add the cabbage. Cook until it begins to wilt. Add the reserved marinade with the garlic, beef stock, salt and pepper; mix well. Add the pork, covering with the cabbage. Cook, covered, over low heat for 10 minutes, turning the pork once.

Remove the pork to a plate. Cook the cabbage, uncovered, until any remaining liquid is reduced to syrup. Adjust the seasonings. Slice the pork. Spoon the cabbage onto plates and arrange the pork on top. Garnish with steamed baby carrots.

155

Veal Scallopine with Mushroom and Sun-Dried Tomato Cream Sauce

6 servings

6 veal cutlets

SAUCE:

6 to 8 sun-dried tomatoes	1/3 c. dry white wine ☺
2 1/2 T. unsalted butter	1/2 to 1 c. whipping cream
1/4 lb. field or porcini mushrooms, sliced	Salt & white pepper

5 T. flour	2 1/2 T. unsalted butter
1 T. freshly-ground pepper	

Pound veal until thickness is reduced by half and cut into 1x2-inch pieces.

Sauce: Place sun-dried tomatoes in a small saucepan and just cover with water. Bring to a boil and simmer for 18 minutes. Drain tomatoes, reserving liquid, and julienne.

Add 2 1/2 tablespoons butter and mushrooms to a large skillet and sauté until just beginning to brown. Add white wine to skillet and boil to reduce to a glaze. Add cream, sun-dried tomatoes and liquid; reduce by 1/3. Season to taste with salt and white pepper. Set aside and keep warm.

Combine flour and black pepper. Flour veal. Melt remaining butter in separate large skillet over medium-high heat and sauté veal 30 seconds on each side.

Arrange veal on platter and spoon sauce over top.

♉ Stuffed Breast of Veal with Wild Rice

4 to 6 servings

1 whole veal breast (have butcher cut pocket in breast)	6 oz. white rice, cooked
	Shallots, minced
3/4 lb. mushrooms, finely minced (extract moisture by squeezing)	Salt & freshly-ground pepper
	Dry white wine, to taste ☺
4 T. butter, melted	Cashew nuts (opt.)
4 oz. wild rice, cooked	Veal or chicken stock

Preheat oven to 350° to 375°. In a skillet, combine mushrooms with butter and cook until golden. Mix wild rice and white rice by hand, adding chopped shallots, salt and pepper to taste. Combine with mushroom mixture for dressing.

Braise veal breast briefly in less than 1/8-inch of dry white wine in deep roasting pan. Just before stuffing, add optional cashew nuts to dressing. Stuff as much dressing as possible into pocket of veal breast. If there is additional dressing, bake in a separate casserole, keeping moist with stock.

Roast, loosely covered, adding stock as needed with small amounts of white wine. Roast for 25 to 30 minutes per pound, or until meat thermometer reaches 170°. Uncover and roast 10 to 15 minutes to brown.

♀ Rack of lamb with Fig and Port Wine Sauce

Two 8-rib (2 lb.) lamb rib roasts
Salt
1 1/3 c. port wine ☺
2 T. salad oil
1 sm. onion, minced
1 garlic clove, minced
2 T. all-purpose flour

10 dried figs, each cut in half
1/2 tsp. browning & seasoning
  sauce (opt.)
1/2 c. walnuts, coarsely chopped &
  toasted
Minced parsley, for garnish

Preheat oven to 375°. Rub each lamb rib roast with 1/2 teaspoon salt. In large 10 1/2 x 15 1/2-inch roasting pan, place lamb rib roasts, meat-side up. Insert meat thermometer into center of a roast, making sure pointed end of thermometer does not touch bone. Roast lamb 40 minutes, or until meat thermometer reaches 140° for rare, or until desired doneness. When roasts are done, remove to a large platter. Let stand 15 minutes, for easier carving.

Meanwhile, prepare sauce.

Sauce: Add 1 cup water to drippings in roasting pan. Stir until brown bits are loosened; pour mixture through sieve into 4-cup measuring cup. Skim off fat, if any, from drippings mixture. Add port wine and enough water to equal 3 1/2 cups.

In 3-quart saucepan over medium-high heat, in hot salad oil, cook onion and garlic until tender, but not browned. Stir in flour; cook 1 minute. Stir in port-wine mixture, figs, browning and seasoning sauce and 1/2 teaspoon salt. Over high heat, heat to boiling. Reduce heat to medium-low; simmr 10 minutes, or until figs are tender and sauce thickens slightly.

To serve, spoon sauce around lamb. Sprinkle with toasted walnuts. Garnish lamb with parsley.

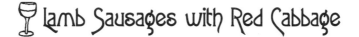

� lamb Sausages with Red Cabbage

2 servings

3 lamb sausages or mild Italian
  sausages
3 c. thinly-sliced red cabbage
1/4 c. chopped onion
1/4 c. chopped green apple

1/3 c. medium-bodied red wine ☺
3 T. creme de cassis (black currant-
  flavored liqueur) ☺
3/4 tsp. balsamic vinegar

Combine cabbage, onion, apple, wine and cassis in a heavy stockpot. Bring to a boil, then reduce heat and cover pot. Simmer until tender, stirring occasionally, 30 to 40 minutes. Remove from heat and stir in the vinegar. Grill or sauté the sausages.

To serve, divide the braised cabbage between 2 plates and place sausage on top. Accompany with steamed new potatoes, a green salad, and a good red wine.

"If you want breakfast in bed, sleep in the kitchen."
          --Unknown

Braised lamb Shanks

Serves 4

Cook in your crock-pot. Easy.

1 yellow onion, diced	1 tsp. chopped fresh thyme
2 celery stalks, diced	1 bay leaf
2 carrots, peeled & diced	4 lamb shanks, external fat
3 garlic cloves, crushed	trimmed
2 c. chicken stock	Salt & freshly-ground pepper, to
1 c. peeled, seeded & chopped	taste
tomatoes	2 T. olive oil
2 T. tomato paste	1 1/4 c. red wine ☺

Put the onion, celery, carrots, garlic, stock, 1 cup peeled, seeded and chopped tomatoes, tomato paste, thyme and bay leaf in a slow cooker and stir to combine. Season the lamb shanks with salt and pepper. In a large sauté pan over medium-high heat, warm the olive oil until nearly smoking. Add the shanks and brown on all sides, about 5 minutes total. Transfer to a slow cooker. Remove the sauté pan from the heat, pour in the wine and return to medium-high heat. Bring to a simmer, stirring to scrape up any browned bits from the pan bottom. Add the wine to the slow cooker, cover and cook on high for 6 hours according to the manufacturer's instructions. Transfer the lamb shanks to a large serving dish. Remove the bay leaf from the cooking liquid. Using a blender or stick blender, purée the liquids and solids until smooth. Pour some of the sauce over the shanks and pass the rest alongside.

♀ Roast leg of lamb with Rosemary

6 servings

6 lb. leg of lamb	**2 leeks, sliced**
Salt & pepper	**2 T. butter**
3/4 tsp. rosemary	**2 c. dry Sauterne** ☺
1 carrot, sliced	**2 c. water**
1 stalk celery, chopped	

Place leg of lamb in a roasting pan and sprinkle with salt and pepper and 1/4 teaspoon rosemary. Cook carrot, celery and leeks in saucepan with butter for 5 minutes, stirring frequently. Add 1/2 cup Sauterne and 1/2 cup water. Remove from heat. Pour vegetables and liquid around the lamb. Roast at 325° for 2 1/2 to 3 hours, adding wine and water in equal proportions as necessary. Baste occasionally after the first hour of cooking. When lamb is cooked, remove to a hot platter and keep warm. Skim off fat in roaster and add 1 cup Sauterne, 1 cup water and 1/2 teaspoon rosemary. Season with salt and pepper. Thicken, if you wish, with a flour paste. Strain gravy and serve with roast.

Braised Lamb Shanks with Sour Cream and Capers

2 lamb shanks, each cracked into 3
  pieces
2 T. meat drippings or cooking oil
3/4 tsp. salt
1/2 c. dry white or red wine ☺

1 bay leaf & 1 sprig each of parsley
  & thyme, tied in cheesecloth
  (bouquet garni)
1/2 c. sour cream
2 T. capers

Brown shanks well in drippings in a heavy kettle over moderate heat; pour off drippings. Add remaining ingredients. Cover and simmer about 1 1/2 hours, turning shanks once or twice, until tender. Or cover and bake about 1 1/2 hours at 325°.

Lift shanks to a deep platter. Skim fat from broth, mix in sour cream and capers. Spoon a little sauce over shanks and pass the rest.

"I like work; it fascinates me. I can sit and look at it for hours."
--Jerome K. Kerome

Veal Scallopine Alla Marsala

4 servings

An Italian favorite, the dish is easy to prepare.

4 flattened slices veal cutlet	**Salt & pepper**
Grated Parmesan cheese	**1/3 to 1/2 c. Marsala wine** ☺
1/4 c. butter	**1 tsp. demi-glaze**

Dip the cleaver-flattened, thin slices of meat into grated cheese, and sauté in butter until browned on each side. Season with salt and pepper. Transfer to hot platter. Add demi-glaze and Marsala to skillet, simmer a few minutes and pour over meat. Serve at once.

One cup diced mushrooms may be sautéed in the butter after the meat.

"The biggest liar in the world is the golfer
who claims he plays the game for exercise."
--Tommy Bolt

♟ leg of lamb with Artichoke Stuffing

4 to 6 servings

STUFFING:

1/2 c. chopped onion

1 or 2 cloves garlic, chopped

2 T. butter or olive oil

1 (15 oz.) can artichoke hearts,
   drained & chopped

1 c. fresh breadcrumbs

1/4 c. chopped fresh parsley

2 or 3 sprigs dill, chopped

Salt & freshly-ground pepper

3 to 3 1/2 lb. leg of lamb, boned

Dry white wine ☺

Stuffing: Sauté onions and garlic in butter for 5 minutes. Add chopped artichoke hearts. Cook 2 to 3 minutes. Remove from heat. Stir in the breadcrumbs, parsley, dill, salt and pepper to taste. Add a little melted butter if stuffing seems too dry. Chill.

Preheat oven to 325°. Open leg of lamb and place stuffing in middle. Roll and tie lamb. Bake for 30 minutes per pound. Baste with a little white wine during the last 30 minutes.

NOTE:

You could take the cold stuffing to the butcher and have him stuff and tie the leg of lamb.

Leg of lamb can also be done easily on a covered grill. Use a meat thermometer to determine cooking time.

Castilian Veal

6 to 8 servings

1 sm. leg of veal, about 4 lb.
3 strips bacon
1 carrot, cut in slivers
1/2 c. olive oil (or salad oil)
1 T. flour
1/3 c. sherry ☺

2 T. water
12 sm. white onions, peeled
1/2 c. green olives, pitted, or
   stuffed olives
1 bay leaf
1/8 tsp. thyme

Insert strips of bacon and slivers of carrot in slits in veal. Salt and pepper the meat. Brown in oil in roasting pan. Stir in flour, add sherry and water. Cover and cook until tender, at 325° about 2 to 2 1/2 hours. After the first hour, add onions, olives, bay leaf and thyme. When ready to serve, slice meat; arrange on a hot platter and garnish with onions and olives.

"Only Irish coffee provides in a single glass all four essential food groups: alcohol, caffeine, sugar and fat."
--Lisa Leslie

(Yum!)

Stuffed Veal Chops Chablis

4 servings

4 veal chops, about 1 1/4" thick
1 1/2 c. soft bread crumbs
1/2 c. ground or minced cooked
  ham
1 T. minced onion
3 T. melted butter
Salt & pepper

Flour
3 T. bacon drippings, or other fat
1 1/2 c. Chablis, Sauterne or other
  white wine ☺
1 can condensed cream of
  mushroom soup

Have each chop slit from fat side to bone to form a pocket. Mix breadcrumbs, ham, onion and butter; season with salt and pepper; stuff chops with the mixture. Skewer openings. Dredge chops with seasoned flour. Brown on both sides in hot drippings; add wine. Cover and simmer gently for 45 minutes, or until chops are very tender. Place on heated platter. Measure 1 cup of skillet liquid, combine with mushroom soup and heat to boiling. Season to taste with salt and pepper and serve with the chops.

 Quick Osso Buco

6 servings

1 T. olive oil
2 lb. bone-in veal shoulder arm
  steaks
1 (16 oz.) bag peeled baby carrots
1/2 (16 oz.) bag frozen sm. onions
1 med. celery stalk, cut crosswise
  into 1/2" pieces
3 garlic cloves, minced

1/2 tsp. salt
1/4 tsp. ground black pepper
1/4 tsp. dried thyme
1 (14 1/2 oz.) can diced tomatoes
1/3 c. dry white wine ☺
1/2 c. loosely-packed fresh parsley
  leaves, chopped
2 tsp. grated fresh lemon peel

In 6-quart pressure cooker, heat oil over high heat. Add half the veal and cook until browned on both sides. Transfer veal to bowl; repeat with remaining veal. Add carrots, onions, celery, garlic, salt, pepper and thyme and cook 1 minute, stirring. Stir in tomatoes, wine and 1/4 cup water; heat (try not to boil) over high heat.

Return veal to pressure cooker. Following manufacturer's directions, cover pressure cooker and bring up to pressure; cook under pressure 15 minutes. Release pressure quickly, as manufacturer directs.

In cup, mix parsley with lemon peel; sprinkle over stew.

♀ Roast Goose with Oranges and Madeira

6 servings

FOR THE GOOSE:
1 (12 lb.) goose, neck reserved
1 T. butter
3 shallots, sliced
1 3/4 c. Madeira wine ☺
4 sm. oranges, quartered
4 c. canned low-salt chicken broth

1 c. fresh orange juice
4 lg. shallots, halved
1/3 c. + 2 T. Madeira wine ☺
1 T. cornstarch
2 T. honey

FOR THE SHALLOTS:
1 T. butter
18 shallots, peeled
1 1/2 c. Madeira wine ☺

3/4 c. canned low-salt chicken
  broth
3 T. honey

To make the goose: Remove excess skin, fat and quills from goose, carefully lower goose into large pot of boiling water. Boil 1 minute. Remove from water. Pat dry. Place on rack in large pan. Chill, uncovered, 2 days.

Melt butter in heavy large saucepan over medium heat. Add goose neck; cook until brown, turning once, about 5 minutes. Add sliced shallots; sauté until tender, about 4 minutes. Add 1 1/2 cups Madeira wine and 1 orange. Cook until reduced by 1/3, scraping up browned bits, about 3 minutes. Add broth and juice. Boil until reduced to 2 cups liquid, about 45 minutes. Strain sauce into saucepan. (Can be made 2 days ahead. Chill.)

Continued on following page.

Continued from preceding page.

Preheat oven to 325°. Pierce goose skin (not meat) all over with fork. Place halved shallots and remaining 3 oranges in cavity of goose. Tie legs together to hold shape. Season with salt and pepper. Place goose, breast-side down, on rack in roasting pan. Roast 1 1/2 hours. Transfer goose to platter.

Pour off fat from pan. Place goose, breast-side up, on rack in pan. Roast until thermometer inserted into thickest part of thigh registers 180°, about 1 hour and 15 minutes. Increase oven temperature to 450°. Roast goose until golden, about 10 minutes. Transfer to platter. Pour off all fat from pan, leaving browned bits in pan. Pour 1/3 cup Madeira wine into pan. Gently heat pan while scraping up browned bits. Pour mixture into sauce. Dissolve cornstarch in remaining Madeira wine. Whisk into sauce. Boil until thickened to sauce consistency, about 7 minutes. Stir in 2 tablespoons honey. Season to taste with more honey, salt and pepper.

To make the shallots: Melt butter in heavy large saucepan over medium heat. Add shallots; sauté until golden, about 10 minutes. Stir in Madeira wine, broth and honey. Simmer until shallots are tender and liquid is reduced to glaze, about 1 hour and 10 minutes. (Glazed shallots can be made 1 day ahead. Cover and refrigerate. Re-warm over low heat, stirring often, before serving.)

Carve goose. Arrange slices on plates. Top with Madeira-glazed shallots and sauce and serve.

Plan 2 days ahead for this one. Another great recipe for the holidays.

Notes & Recipes

Soups, Stews, Sauces, Marinades & Miscellaneous

FAVORITE RECIPES
FROM MY COOKBOOK

Recipe Name	Page Number

🍷 She - Crab Soup

Makes about 1 quart.

1/4 lb. butter
1/2 c. flour
1 lb. real crabmeat
1 pt. milk

1 pt. half & half
1 T. Old Bay seasoning
1/2 c. dry sherry ☺

Combine butter and flour, cooking over low heat for 3 to 4 minutes. Add milk gradually, stirring, and then add seasoning and crabmeat. Simmer on low heat for about 30 minutes when soup becomes the desired consistency. Remove from heat and add sherry and half & half. If desired, garnish with crumbled egg yolks.

🍷 Shrimp Bisque

8 to 10 servings

2 c. flour
1/2 lb. butter
2 qt. water
1 lb. shrimp, cooked & chopped
2 bay leaves
1 onion, chopped

6 stalks celery, chopped
1 T. Old Bay seasoning
1/2 c. dry sherry ☺
1 c. heavy cream, or fat-free half &
    half for less calories
Juice of 1 lemon

Cook shrimp in the water and save the liquid to use as the stock. Make a roux of the flour and butter. Add celery and onion; cook until the vegetables become transparent. Add the stock to roux and cook until thick. Add the shrimp and stir in the sherry and cream. Salt and pepper to taste.

171

🍷 Shrimp and Scallop Stew

4 servings

2 lg. green onions, white & green parts only, washed
2 T. olive oil
2 tsp. chopped garlic, about 3 cloves
1 jalapeño pepper, seeded & finely chopped (or less to taste)
1 med. carrot, peeled & thinly diced
3/4 tsp. ground cumin
1/8 tsp. cayenne pepper

1/4 tsp. ground cinnamon
1 1/2 tsp. salt
1 1/2 c. chopped tomatoes with juice
1 c. dry white wine ☺
1 lb. med. shrimp, shelled, deveined, tail section left on
1 lb. sea scallops or lg. bay scallops, muscle removed
3 T. fresh cilantro leaves, coarsely chopped

Slice leeks in half lengthwise and cut into 1/2-inch dice. In a stockpot, heat oil over medium heat. Add leeks and garlic; sauté, stirring, until translucent, about 7 minutes. Add jalapeño, carrots, spices and salt; lower heat to medium-low and cook until carrots are medium tender, 4 to 5 minutes. Add tomatoes, wine and 1 cup water. Bring to a boil and lower heat to medium; cook 5 minutes. Stir in shrimp and scallops; cook until just opaque, 4 to 6 minutes. Remove from heat. Add cilantro and serve over pasta.

Seafood Pasta Chowder

16 servings

6 oz. mini pasta bow-ties or shells
3 oz. frozen or canned crabmeat
1/3 c. butter or margarine
8 oz. fresh mushrooms, sliced into
  1-inch pieces
2 (1 oz.) pkt. Knorr Newburg sauce
  mix

3 c. milk
1 1/2 c. water
1/3 c. dry white wine ☺
1/4 c. green onions, sliced
Parsley, for garnish

Cook the pasta according to the package directions. Drain and rinse lightly with cold water to prevent it sticking together, and set aside. Sort crabmeat to remove any shell pieces.

Melt butter or margarine in a heavy, 3-qaurt saucepan. Add mushrooms and sauté 3 minutes. Add sauce mix and stir well. Add milk, water and wine. Stir well with a wire whip over moderate heat until the mixture comes to a boil. Reduce the heat and simmer 5 to 8 minutes, stirring constantly. Add the green onions, precooked pasta and crabmeat. Stir to combine. Sprinkle with parsley and serve immediately.

Bouillabaisse

4 to 6 servings

1/4 c. olive oil
4 c. chopped tomatoes
2 T. tomato paste
1 c. chopped onion
3 cloves garlic, minced
1 tsp. salt
1 bay leaf
1/4 tsp. freshly-ground pepper
1/2 tsp. dried basil
1/2 tsp. dried thyme

1/4 tsp. fennel seed
Dash of saffron
2 c. water
1 1/2 doz. sm. clams
1 lb. cod fillets
1/2 lb. king crab pieces
3/4 lb. shrimp, shelled
1/4 c. butter
1 c. dry white wine ☺

Heat oil in large soup pot. Add tomatoes, tomato paste, onion, garlic, salt, pepper, bay leaf, basil, thyme, fennel seed and saffron. Simmer 10 minutes. Add water and clams. Simmer 15 minutes, or until clams open. Add cod fillets, crab, shrimp, butter and wine. Simmer 20 minutes, or until fish flakes.

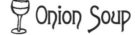

Onion Soup

6 servings

5 c. thinly-sliced onions
1/4 lb. margarine
2 cans consommé
2 cans water
1 c. sherry ☺
2 T. flour

1 T. sugar
1 clove garlic, minced
Chopped parsley
Salt, to taste
1/4 tsp. thyme

TOPPING:
1/4 c. Parmesan cheese   3/4 c. Gueyre cheese

Brown onions lightly in the margarine. Pour off excess margarine. Add the other ingredients and simmer very slowly for 2 hours, covered.

Make a day ahead. Remove hardened fat before warming.

When ready to serve, heat soup to boiling, pour into bake and serve casserole. Cover with 6 slices of toasted French bread. Sprinkle with 1/4 cup Parmesan cheese and 3/4 cup Gueyre cheese. Heat in 275° oven until cheese melts, about 5 minutes.

Cheddar and Bacon Soup

2 quarts

Very good, but I leave out the olives.

5 slices bacon
1/2 c. grated carrots
1/2 c. finely-chopped celery
1/2 c. finely-chopped onion
1/2 c. finely-chopped green pepper
1/4 c. flour
4 c. chicken stock

3 c. shredded sharp Cheddar
cheese
2 c. milk
1 to 2 T. dry sherry
5 oz. pimento-stuffed olives,
chopped
Salt & pepper, to taste

In a large pan, fry bacon until crisp; drain and reserve drippings. Crumble bacon and set aside.

Sauté carrots, celery, onion and green pepper in bacon drippings until tender, not brown. Blend in flour and gradually add stock. Cook over low heat until mixture thickens and boils. Continue cooking about 5 minutes. Add cheese and stir until melted. Stir in milk, sherry and olives. Simmer for 10 minutes. Season to taste and serve garnished with crumbled bacon.

♟ Orange Carrot Bisque

6 servings

1/4 c. unsalted butter	1 c. fresh orange juice
2 c. finely-chopped onion	Freshly-grated orange zest
1 1/2 lb. carrots, pared & chopped	1/3 c. Grand Marnier ☺
4 c. chicken broth, divided	Salt & freshly-ground pepper

GARNISH:

Whipping cream, whipped, or sour cream	Freshly-ground nutmeg
	Fresh parsley

Melt butter in a large, heavy saucepan. Add onions and stir well. Cover and cook over low heat for 25 minutes, or until onions are golden. Stir occasionally. Add carrots and chicken broth. Bring to a boil, reduce heat and simmer, covered, for 30 to 35 minutes, or until carrots are tender.

Drain mixture in sieve over large bowl, reserving the broth. Purée vegetables in a food processor or blender with 1 cup of reserved broth. Return the purée to cleaned pan. Stir in orange juice and enough of the reserved broth to thin the soup to desired consistency. Add orange zest and Grand Marnier.

Add salt and pepper to taste. Heat soup over moderately-low heat, stirring until it is just heated through. Ladle soup into bowls and garnish with a dollop of unsweetened, stiffly-whipped cream or sour cream, topped with a grind of fresh nutmeg. Sprinkle with chopped fresh parsley.

Fresh Mushroom Soup

6 servings

1 lb. mushrooms, 1/3 sliced, 2/3 finely chopped (can use shiitake, button or mix any kind together)
6 T. butter
2 c. finely-chopped onions
1/2 tsp. sugar
1/4 c. flour

1 c. water (can use 1/2 c. water & 1/2 c. milk or 1 c. cream for thicker soup)
1 3/4 c. chicken broth
1 c. dry vermouth ☺
1 T. salt (or to taste)
1/4 tsp. freshly-ground pepper (or to taste)

In large saucepan, melt butter. Add onions and sugar. Sauté over medium heat, stirring frequently, for about 15 minutes, or until golden. Add sliced and chopped mushrooms and sauté for 4 minutes. Stir in flour until smooth; cook for 2 minutes, stirring constantly. Pour in water and stir until smooth. Add chicken broth, vermouth, salt and pepper; heat to boiling, stirring constantly. Reduce heat and simmer, uncovered, 10 minutes.

May be prepared in advance, refrigerated and reheated to boiling.

"A bargain is something you cannot use at a price you cannot resist."
--Unknown
(Like the clothes in the back of my closet that
I was going to lose weight to get into them.) BJ

Black Bean Soup

4 to 6 servings

Good and rich!

1 c. black beans	Dash of red pepper
8 c. water	2 cloves
1/8 tsp. mace	2 hard-cooked eggs, sliced thin
1 carrot, cut in pieces	3 T. sherry☺ (or can use lemon
1 onion, cut in pieces	juice)
1 sm. ham bone, or 1/8 lb. salt pork	1/2 lemon, sliced thin
1/4 lb. beef stew meat, cut in small pieces	

Wash beans, cover with 2 cups water and soak overnight. In the morning, drain water and discard. Put carrot, onion and 2 cups water in blender container, or food processor, cover and process at high speed on and off quickly several times to chop vegetables coarsely. Pour into large saucepan. Add beans and remaining water, meat and seasoning. Cover and cook slowly about 3 hours, or until beans are very soft. Remove meat and cloves. Cool soup slightly. Pour soup through a strainer, reserving stock. Put vegetables into blender container, add stock to cover. Cover container and process at low speed to start, then turn control to high and process until smooth. If mixture is too thick, add a little stock. Return puréed mixture, meat and reserved stock to soup kettle; add sherry or lemon juice and reheat.

You can top with chopped onions, chopped cooked eggs and/or lemon slices.

🍷 Potato Soup with Wine

4 servings

2 slices bacon, cut fine
2 onions, chopped
4 med. potatoes, diced
2 bouillon cubes in 3 c. hot water
1 bay leaf

2 T. chopped parsley
2 c. milk or milk & cream
1/3 c. white wine ☺
Salt & paprika

Cook bacon. Add onions and cook until yellow. Add potatoes, bouillon and bay leaf. Cook until potatoes are tender. Stir in parsley, milk and wine. Adjust seasonings and serve with croutons.

🍷 Sun - Dried Tomatoes Beef Stew

4 servings

1 T. olive oil
2 lb. boneless beef, cut in 1/2"
  cubes
1 lg. onion, finely-chopped

1 c. beef broth or water
1 c. dry red wine ☺
1/2 c. sun-dried tomatoes in olive
  oil

Heat oil in large skillet and brown beef in single layer in 2 or 3 batches. Transfer beef to Dutch oven as it browns. Salt and pepper each batch to taste. Reducing heat, in same pan, sauté onions until tender and clear. Add broth or water and scrape bottom of pan to dissolve all browned bits. Transfer all to Dutch oven. Add wine and sun-dried tomatoes. Bring to boil. Reduce to slow simmer and cook, covered, about 2 hours, or until beef is tender. Add vegetables of your choice, and cook, covered, until vegetables are of desired doneness.

Parsley Soup

2 to 4 servings

1 c. sour cream	1 sm. clove garlic, minced
1 c. whipping cream	2 T. butter
2 lg. bunches parsley, stems removed & minced	2 c. chicken broth
2 T. minced onion	2/3 c. dry white wine ☺
	1 tsp. salt

In a small bowl, mix sour cream and whipping cream. Cover and let set at room temperature. Measure 1 1/2 cups loosely-packed parsley and reserve 2 tablespoons more.

In saucepan over medium heat, melt butter and sauté onion and garlic until onion is translucent, about 5 minutes. Add parsley and cook for 3 minutes, stirring constantly. Pour in chicken broth; cover, reduce heat and simmer 10 minutes. Stir in wine and salt.

Purée in blender or food processor, 2 cups at a time, or press through a sieve. Return purée to heat, bring to boil, remove from heat and stir in 3/4 of the cream mixture.

Serve with dollop of remaining sour cream and whipping cream mixture.

♷ Chicken Stew in White Wine

Serves 4

Use your crock-pot and go shopping.

1/3 c. all-purpose flour
Salt & freshly-ground pepper, to
   taste
1 (3 to 4 lb.) chicken, cut into 8
   serving pieces
3 T. extra-virgin olive oil
3 bacon slices, chopped
1 yellow onion, thinly-sliced
8 oz. white button mushrooms,
   quartered

1 lb. red-skinned potatoes, cut into
   1/2" pieces
3 garlic cloves, crushed
4 fresh, flat-leaf, parsley sprigs
3 fresh thyme sprigs
1 bay leaf
1 1/2 c. chicken broth (use
   homemade stock, if possible)
1 to 2 c. white wine ☺

In a large bowl, combine the flour, salt and pepper. Add the chicken and toss to coat evenly.

In a large sauté pan over medium-high heat, warm half of the olive oil until just smoking. Add half of the chicken and brown on all sides, 3 to 4 minutes total. Transfer to slow-cooker. Repeat with the remaining oil and chicken. Add the bacon, onion, mushrooms, potatoes, garlic, parsley, thyme, bay leaf and chicken broth to the slow-cooker and stir to combine.

Remove the sauté pan from the heat, pour the wine into the pan and return to medium-high heat. Bring to a simmer, stirring to scrape up any browned bits from the pan bottom. Add the wine to the slow-cooker, cover and cook on high for 5 hours according to the manufacturer's instructions. Remove the bay leaf before serving. Spoon the stew into bowls and serve immediately.

Beef Stew

4 servings

1/4 c. olive oil
1 1/2 lb. boneless beef chuck, cut
  into 1 1/2" cubes
2 T. all-purpose flour
12 oz. sm. white boiling onions,
  peeled
1 lb. tomatoes, peeled, seeded &
  chopped
3 garlic cloves, minced
2 1/2 T. chopped fresh thyme, or
  1 tsp. dried thyme

2 1/2 T. chopped fresh rosemary, or
  1 tsp. dried rosemary
2 1/2 T. chopped fresh oregano, or
  1 tsp. dried oregano
1 bay leaf, crumbled
1 tsp. ground cumin
2 to 3 c. dry red wine ☺
1/2 lb. Feta cheese, crumbled
Salt & freshly-ground pepper

Preheat oven to 350°. Heat oil in a heavy 4 to 5-quart Dutch oven over medium-high heat. Toss beef with flour in large bowl. Add beef to pan in batches and cook until brown, stirring occasionally, about 3 minutes per batch. Transfer browned beef to bowl. Add onions to pan and cook until light brown, stirring frequently, about 5 minutes. Add tomatoes, garlic, herbs and cumin to pan. Stir in wine and bring to a boil. Cover and bake in oven until beef is tender, about 2 hours. (Can be prepared 1 day ahead. Cover and refrigerate. Rewarm to 350° before continuing.)

Stir Feta cheese into stew. Return to oven and continue baking until cheese is heated through, about 10 minutes. Season with salt and pepper, and serve.

Beef Stew

6 servings

Put in your slow-cooker and go shopping!

3 lb. boneless stewing beef, cut in 1" cubes
1/3 c. all-purpose flour
Salt & freshly-ground pepper, to taste
3 T. olive oil
1 lg. yellow onion, peeled & finely chopped
2 garlic cloves, crushed
2 carrots, peeled & finely chopped
2 celery stalks, finely chopped
8 oz. new potatoes, cut in 1/2" pieces
1 c. steamed chestnuts
1 T. tomato paste
1 c. beef stock
2 c. red wine ☺

In a large bowl, toss the beef with the flour, salt and pepper to coat evenly.

In a large sauté pan over medium-high heat, warm 1/2 the olive oil until just smoking. Add 1/2 the beef and brown on all sides, 3 to 4 minutes total. Transfer to slow-cooker. Repeat with the remaining oil and beef. Add the onion, garlic, carrots, celery, potatoes, chestnuts, tomato paste and stock to the slow-cooker and stir to combine.

Off the heat, pour the wine into the sauté pan and set over medium-high heat. Bring to a simmer, stirring with a wooden spoon to scrape up the browned bits from the pan bottom. Add the wine to the slow-cooker, cover and cook on high for 6 hours.

Sun-Dried Tomato Spaghetti Sauce

4 servings

8 oz. oil-packed sun-dried
  tomatoes, undrained
1 c. chopped onion
1 c. chopped celery
1 c. diced carrots
3 cloves garlic, minced

2 (28 oz.) cans whole tomatoes,
  undrained
1/2 to 1 c. Chablis or other dry
  white wine (depending on how
  you like your sauce) ☺
1 tsp. dried fennel seed
1/2 tsp. pepper

Drain dried tomatoes, reserving 1/4 cup oil. Chop tomatoes and set aside. Heat reserved oil in a Dutch oven; sauté onion, celery, carrot and garlic in hot oil 15 minutes, stirring occasionally. Stir in dried and canned tomatoes, Chablis, fennel seeds and pepper; cook, uncovered, over medium heat 1 hour, or to desired consistency, stirring mixture occasionally. Position knife blade in food processor bowl; add 1/2 of sauce mixture. Pulse 4 or 5 times, or until mixture is chopped but not smooth. Repeat the same procedure with remaining 1/2 of sauce mixture. Serve over hot pasta.

♟ Red or White Wine Marinade

Makes about 5 cups

This recipe can be made with red wine for beef and lamb or white wine for poultry. Large roasts and whole chickens can marinate for 1 to 3 days; the longer they marinate, the more flavor they will gain.

1 btl. (about 3 1/2 c.) dry red or white wine ☺
1/2 c. olive oil
1 yellow onion, finely chopped
1/4 c. chopped fresh flat-leaf parsley
2 lg. garlic cloves, minced

1 to 2 T. chopped fresh thyme, rosemary, or tarragon, or 2 tsp. dried herb of choice (depending on how large the roast is or if you are marinating more than 1 chicken)
1 tsp. salt
1/2 tsp. freshly-ground pepper

In a large bowl, whisk together the wine, olive oil, onion, parsley, garlic, thyme, salt and pepper. Use immediately or refrigerate in a tightly-covered jar for up to 2 days.

(Enough for a large roast, leg of lamb or whole chicken).

186

♈ Béarnaise Sauce

1/3 c. white wine ☺
2 T. tarragon vinegar
1 tsp. dried tarragon
1 T. chopped shallots

1/4 tsp. pepper
1/4 tsp. salt
1 c. hollandaise sauce

Combine all ingredients in a small pan and bring to a boil. Cook rapidly until the liquid is reduced to about 2 tablespoons or less. Pour this into 1 cup hollandaise and blend until smooth.

Great with beef tenderloin or even cheaper cuts of beef.

♈ Hollandaise Sauce

2 egg yolks
3 T. lemon juice

1/2 c. butter

Whisk yolks and lemon juice until combined. Cut butter into 8 pieces; place 4 in the pan. Melt butter, stirring constantly. Add each of the other 4 pieces of butter as the sauce cooks. Keep stirring. <u>Do not boil</u>! Remove from heat as soon as the butter is all melted.

Great with vegetables!

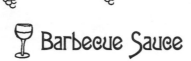

Barbecue Sauce

Makes about 8 quarts.

1 1/2 c. dark brown sugar
1 1/2 c. Worcestershire sauce
1 1/2 c. prepared mustard
1 qt. ketchup
1/2 c. freshly-ground black pepper

1/2 c. crushed red pepper flakes (or
  a little less if you do not like a
  spicy hot sauce)
3 qt. red wine vinegar
2 qt. water
1 qt. white wine ☺
1 1/2 c. salt

Place all the ingredients in a 12-quart stainless steel pot and bring to a boil. Reduce the heat to a low simmer, cover, and cook for 30 minutes. Store, covered, in the refrigerator.

Can use as a marinade sauce as well as barbecue sauce. You can also use this as a base for Bloody Mary's.

 Beurre Blanc

Makes about 1 cup.

1/4 c. white wine ☺
1/4 c. cider vinegar
1 T. minced shallot

3/4 to 1 lb. cold unsalted butter
Salt & freshly-ground pepper

VARIATION NO. 1:
1/4 c. orange juice

Zest of 1 orange

VARIATION NO. 2:
1/2 c. pineapple juice
1/4 c. white wine vinegar
1/4 c. minced green onion

1/2 tsp. salt
1/4 tsp. freshly-ground white
   pepper

Combine wine, vinegar and shallot in saucepan. Reduce over high heat to 2 tablespoons. Cut butter into 1-inch cubes. Over very low heat, whisk into reduction. When smooth emulsion forms, remove from heat. Add salt and pepper to taste. Serve with green vegetables, shellfish or fish.

Variation No. 1: Add orange juice and orange zest to reduction. Then add butter. Serve over fish, veal or chicken.

Variation No. 2: Reduce pineapple juice, vinegar, onion, salt and pepper. Add butter. Serve over asparagus, broccoli, beans, scallops or chicken.

♈ Peach Sauce

1/2 c. peach preserves, 1/2 c. apricot preserves

1 c. peeled & diced peaches
2 T. orange liqueur ☺

Heat peach or apricot preserves. Stir in 1 cup of peaches and liqueur. Chill.

♈ Raspberry Sauce

1/2 c. currant jelly
1 c. raspberries

2 T. dry red wine ☺

Heat jelly. Stir in raspberries and wine. Chill.

Sherried French Toast

4 to 6 servings

There are 3 ways to cook this sophisticated dish.

3 eggs, beaten with 1/2 c. milk, 1/2 c. sherry ☺ & 1/2 tsp. salt

6 to 10 slices bread, crusts trimmed if you like, cut in halves if you like

Place egg mixture in shallow dish and dip bread into it, allowing it to soak. Let drain a second or two, then sauté in butter in a heavy skillet, turning when golden brown underneath, or fry in deep-fat at 365° until golden, or bake on a buttered cookie sheet at 450° for 8 to 10 minutes. Turn and bake 5 minutes longer.

Serve with butter and maple syrup, jelly or jam. Wonderful with applesauce. Slices may be dipped in confectioners' sugar after French frying.

Scrambled Eggs with Chablis

4 servings

6 eggs
1/4 c. cream
1/4 c. Chablis or any white table wine ☺

1/2 tsp. salt
Few grains of pepper
2 T. butter
1 (3 oz.) pkg. cream cheese, cubed

Beat eggs lightly. Add cream, Chablis, salt and pepper. Melt butter in skillet, chafing dish or double boiler. When hot, pour in the egg mixture. Stir occasionally until eggs are almost firm, still very moist. Stir in the cheese and serve without further cooking.

Swiss Cheese Pie

6 servings

PIE CRUST:

1 1/2 c. flour	9 T. butter
1/8 tsp. salt	1 egg

FILLING:

1/2 lb. aged Swiss cheese, thinly-
   sliced or shredded

2 green onions, with about 3" of
   green tops, thinly sliced

3 eggs

1 c. cream

1/4 c. white wine ☺

1/2 clove garlic, crushed fine

1/4 tsp. freshly-ground black
   pepper

Nutmeg

Sift flour and salt for crust into mixing bowl. With a pastry blender or 2 knives, cut butter into dry ingredients until particles are fine. Add beaten egg and toss with fork until thoroughly blended. Press mixture into bottom and sides of 9-inch pie pan. Prick all over with floured fork. Bake at 425° for 20 minutes, or until golden brown. Cool on rack.

Filling: Arrange Swiss cheese over bottom of cooled shell. Sprinkle with onions. Beat together the eggs, cream, wine, garlic and pepper until thoroughly mixed. Pour into shell and sprinkle lightly with nutmeg. Bake at 325° for 50 to 55 minutes, or until custard is set and barely tinged with brown. Cut into wedges and serve immediately with chilled white wine (the kind used in the pie) and a salad.

Cheddar Cheese Spread with Port

1 cup

Use the sharpest Cheddar you can find.

1/4 c. port or sherry ☺
2 T. cream
1/4 tsp. paprika
Dash of onion salt
1/2 lb. sharp Cheddar cheese, diced

Put everything into your electric blender or food processor, and mix smooth. The cheese can be molded in a small bowl by chilling it.

Brainless French Bread

1 loaf

Garlic may be added, if you like. Either way, this is great with spaghetti.

1 long loaf French bread
1/2 c. soft butter
1/4 c. red wine ☺
1/2 c. grated Parmesan cheese

Cut bread not quite through the loaf in thickish slices. Spread whipped-together mixture of butter, wine and cheese between slices and over bread. A crushed clove of garlic and a sprinkle of mixed salad herbs may be added to the spread. Bake at 400° for 10 minutes, or until hot.

Notes & Recipes

Desserts

FAVORITE RECIPES
FROM MY COOKBOOK

Recipe Name	Page Number

Glazed Bananas

6 to 8 servings

8 bananas, slightly underripe
3 c. sugar
1 1/2 c. wine vinegar

2/3 c. Burgundy or dry red wine ☺
1 T. whole cloves
2 tsp. cinnamon

In a large skillet, combine sugar, vinegar, wine, cloves and cinnamon. Bring mixture to a boil. Drop bananas in mixture, turning once. Cook approximately 2 to 3 minutes, until bananas are well-glazed, tender on the outside but firm inside.

Serve as a side dish with steaks, roasts or fowl, or serve as a dessert and add vanilla ice cream. Excellent for brunch.

Strawberry Amaretto

2 pt. fresh strawberries, stemmed
2 c. sour cream
1 c. packed brown sugar

1/2 c. Amaretto ☺
1 c. whipping cream, whipped

Cut strawberries in half. Mix strawberries, sour cream, brown sugar and Amaretto together the day before serving. Refrigerate. Occasionally stir mixture and keep refrigerated.

Serve strawberries with sauce in balloon glasses or crystal bowls and top with a dollop of whipped cream, or serve over best quality French vanilla ice cream.

🍷 Peach, Honey and Cardamom Wine Cordial

6 to 8 servings

Make this special cordial when fresh peaches are at their best. Serve it in the garden after a summer dinner.

5 lg. ripe peaches, peeled	**1/2 c. Italian honey**
1 btl. dry white wine ☺	**3/4 c. vodka ☺**
8 cardamom pods	

Place the whole peaches in a large glass jar. Add the wine and cardamom pods, the wine should cover the peaches fully. Cover the jar and let stand at room temperature overnight, then refrigerate for 4 days.

Strain the wine into a nonaluminum saucepan. Place over low heat, add the honey and stir just until the honey dissolves, about 5 minutes. Remove from the heat and let cool. Stir in the vodka. Ladle the liqueur into a clean glass bottle or jar. Cover and refrigerate until well chilled, about 2 hours. Serve chilled. It will keep for up to 1 month in the refrigerator.

🍷 Sherried Baked Cranberry Sauce

6 to 8 servings

1 c. sherry ☺	**1/4 tsp. salt**
1 c. sugar	**1 (16 oz.) pkg. cranberries**
1 T. grated orange zest (opt.)	

Preheat oven to 350°. In a large saucepan, bring sherry, sugar, orange zest and salt to a boil. Add cranberries. Pour into a 1-quart baking dish. Bake for 30 minutes. Cool and refrigerate.

Baked Apples Marsala

6 servings

2 c. apple cider
1 1/4 c. dry Marsala wine ☺
1/4 c. + 6 T. firmly-packed light
  brown sugar
6 nice-size baking apples
2 T. golden raisins

2 T. raisins
2 T. dried currants
2 T. chopped almonds
1 1/2 T. margarine
1/4 tsp. freshly-grated nutmeg

In a heavy saucepan over medium heat, combine the cider and Marsala and boil until reduced to 1 cup, about 20 minutes. Stir in the 1/4 cup brown sugar. The syrup can be made 1 day ahead. Cover and refrigerate, then bring to room temperature before using.

Preheat oven to 350°. Peel the top one-fourth of each apple and core them without cutting through the bottom. Place the apples in a ceramic baking dish. Spoon 1 tablespoon brown sugar and 1 teaspoon each of the golden raisins, raisins, currants and almonds into each apple. Pour the syrup over and around the apples. Top each one with 1/4 tablespoon margarine, then sprinkle with the nutmeg. Cover the dish with aluminum foil and bake for 30 minutes. Uncover and continue baking, basting the apples frequently with the syrup, until tender, about 25 minutes more. Transfer the apples to shallow bowls and spoon some of the syrup around each apple. Serve hot or warm.

🍷 Glazed Oranges in Cointreau

8 to 10 servings

SYRUP:
2 c. water
2 c. sugar
1/4 tsp. cream of tartar

1/2 c. cointreau, Grand Marnier or
  rum ☺
1 T. grenadine ☺

8 lg. navel oranges

  Syrup: Remove orange zest, without white, from oranges. Cut into fine slivers. Put slivers in saucepan with water, sugar and cream of tartar. Bring to a boil, then reduce heat to simmer and cook until thick and syrupy, about 25 to 30 minutes. Remove from heat; stir in liqueur, then add grenadine. Chill.

  Oranges: Finish peeling oranges. Either leave whole, slice or section for easier eating. Place in glass bowl, add syrup, distributing peel evenly. Refrigerate, covered, for at least 2 hours.

  Serve with Florentines or brandy snaps filled with vanilla-flavored whipped cream.

Flaming Bananas

4 servings

4 T. butter	**1/4 c. rum** ☺
1/2 c. brown sugar	**1/8 c. banana liqueur** ☺
2 lg. bananas, sliced	**Vanilla ice cream**

In a large skillet, melt butter. Stir in brown sugar and bananas. Pour rum and liqueur into long-handled container and warm slightly. Ignite rum and liqueur mixture and pour gently over banana mixture. Stir gently and spoon over vanilla ice cream served in sherbet glasses.

A fourteenth-century mural in a Swiss carnotset tells a Greek legend in these words:
When men began to drink
They burst into song, like birds.
When they drank more
They became strong as lions,
When they drank too much
They became stupid as asses.
          (And nothing has changed with them since the 14th century!)

Hot Fruit Compote

8 servings

Almost any combination of fruit you can think of makes delicious dessert this way.

1 (1 lb. 13 oz.) can pineapple slices
1 (1 lb. 13 oz.) can peach halves
1 (1 lb. 13 oz.) can pear halves
1 (1 lb. 13 oz.) can light sweet cherries
2 oranges, sectioned
1 c. fresh seedless grapes or halved seeded green grapes

2/3 c. brown sugar
1/4 c. butter
1 (7 oz.) pkg. coconut macaroons, crumbled
1/2 c. toasted & slivered almonds
1 1/4 c. cream sherry or other dessert wine ☺

Drain the canned fruits; arrange the fruits in layers in a casserole, sprinkling each layer with brown sugar, dotting with butter and then adding a layer of macaroon crumbs. Sprinkle toasted, slivered almonds on top and add sherry. Place fruit in a 375° oven, turn off heat and leave while you eat the first course.

 Lazy Daisy Cake

9 to 10 servings

Serve this cake warm - it's so good!

1 pkg. white or yellow cake mix
3 T. butter
6 T. brown sugar
2 T. cream

2 T. muscatel ☺
1/2 c. shredded coconut
1/4 c. chopped nuts

Mix the cake as the package directs and bake it in a 9x9x2-inch pan. Mix butter, sugar, cream, muscatel, coconut and nuts. When the cake comes out of the oven, spread with the mixture and place cake under broiler unit, just long enough to lightly brown and bubble the topping.

"Seize the moment. Remember all those women on the Titanic who waved off the dessert cart."
--Erma Bombeck

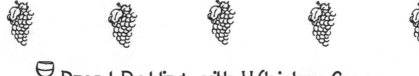

Bread Pudding with Whiskey Cream

10 to 12 servings

1 (16 oz.) loaf stale French bread
  with crust, sliced 1" thick
1 c. butter
2 c. sugar
8 eggs

4 c. milk
2 tsp. cinnamon
2 T. vanilla extract
1/2 c. raisins
1 c. pecans, toasted

WHISKEY CREAM SAUCE:
7 egg yolks
2 c. sugar

1 1/2 c. half & half
4 T. whiskey (or to taste) ☺

VANILLA SAUCE:
2 c. whipping cream
1/2 c. sugar
4 egg yolks
1 T. all-purpose flour

1 T. vanilla extract
1/4 tsp. salt
2 scoops French vanilla ice cream

Butter a 9x13-inch baking pan and place half of bread slices on bottom of dish. Cream butter and sugar. Add eggs and milk, followed by remaining ingredients and mix well. Pour 1/2 of sauce over bread slices. Place the remaining slices in baking dish and pour remaining sauce slowly on top. Let stand 30 minutes.

Preheat oven to 375°. Bake, covered, for 30 minutes. Uncover and bake 15 minutes longer, or until golden. Slice pudding while still warm and serve with Whiskey Cream or Vanilla Sauce.

Continued on following page.

Continued from preceding page.

Whiskey Cream Sauce: Beat sugar into egg yolks until pale in color. Heat half & half until scalding. Remove from heat and very slowly whisk in egg/sugar mixture. Return to low heat and cook until thickened, stirring constantly. Cool over ice and slowly add whiskey.

Vanilla Sauce: In a 2-quart saucepan, combine cream and sugar. Bring to a boil. Remove from heat. In a bowl, whisk together egg yolks, flour, vanilla and salt. Stir in a little hot cream mixture. Add this mixture to the remaining hot cream, and return to heat, stirring constantly until thickened. Do not overcook. Remove from heat and add ice cream, stirring until melted. Strain. Sauce may be served hot or cold.

Eggnog Refrigerator Cake

8 servings

A pretty party dessert that is rich but not too sweet. You might add color by garnishing with maraschino cherries.

1 T. (env.) plain gelatin
1/4 c. cold water
4 eggs, separated
1/2 c. sherry or port ☺
1/4 c. sugar

1 c. cream, whipped
1 tsp. vanilla
10 ladyfingers, split
12 almond macaroons, crumbled

Soften gelatin in cold water, dissolve over boiling water. Beat egg yolks until light; add sherry gradually, beating constantly. Add gelatin mixture and blend. Beat egg whites until stiff. Add sugar gradually, beating after each addition. Fold into yolk mixture. Fold in whipped cream and vanilla. Line loaf pan with split ladyfingers, and alternate layers of eggnog mixture with macaroon crumbs in pan. Chill at least 12 hours. Unmold and spread top and sides with additional whipped cream.

Fast, simple and brainless.

 Glazed Strawberry Pie

9-inch pie, 6 pieces

1 qt. ripe strawberries
3/4 c. sugar
1/2 c. water
1/2 c. port ☺

2 1/2 T. cornstarch
1/4 c. sugar
1/8 tsp. salt
Baked pastry shell

Wash and stem strawberries, reserving 1 cup of the poorest for the glaze. Cook this cup of berries with the 3/4 cup sugar, the water and port for 5 minutes. Put through a sieve. Add cornstarch with 1/4 cup sugar and salt. Cook until thick, and let cool. Fill shell with rest of berries, whole or halved. Pour glaze over pie and chill before serving.

The pie is both beautiful and delicious and doesn't need further glamorizing, but of course you may add whipped cream.

Port Wine Cake

9x9x2-inch cake

1/2 c. butter
1 c. sugar
2 tsp. baking powder
1/8 tsp. salt

1 3/4 c. sifted cake flour
1/2 c. port ☺
Grated rind of 1 lemon
4 egg whites, beaten stiff

Cream butter and sugar well. Sift baking powder, salt and cake flour. Add alternately with port to creamed mixture. Add lemon rind. Beat egg whites until stiff and fold them into the batter. Bake cake in an oiled, floured pan at 350° for about 45 minutes.

Frost with a lemon butter icing.

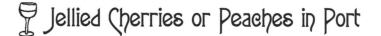

♱ Jellied Cherries or Peaches in Port

6 servings

Two to four times this recipe makes an exciting buffet mold.

1/2 c. port ☺
1 c. sliced fresh pitted dark sweet
   cherries, or sliced fresh or
   canned peaches

1 pkg. strawberry-flavored gelatin
1 1/2 c. hot water

Pour port over fruit and let stand while preparing gelatin. Dissolve gelatin in hot water. Cool and add fruit and port. Chill until slightly thickened, then turn into large mold or individual molds and chill until firm. Serve plain or with chilled soft custard, sour cream or whipped cream.

Variations: Pears may be used in the same recipe. Seedless grapes, port and orange-flavored gelatin are another good combination.

♱ Wine Baked Peaches

6 servings

6 ripe peaches, peeled & sliced
1 T. butter
1/2 tsp. mace
1/2 c. water

1 c. sugar
1 lemon, juice & grated rind
1/3 c. white port ☺

Place peaches in a baking dish which has a cover. Add other ingredients, cover and bake at 375°, until fruit is tender, 1/2 hour or longer. Chill before serving.

Vodka Puddin' Cake

10 to 12 servings

1 box Duncan Hines yellow cake
  mix
1 (3.4 oz.) and 1 (5.9 oz.) box
  chocolate pudding mix
4 eggs, room temp., beaten

1 c. oil
1/2 c. kahlua ☺
1/2 c. good vodka ☺
1 ctn. store-bought chocolate-
  fudge icing

Preheat oven to 350°. Combine in the bowl of your mixer, the cake mix, chocolate pudding mixes and eggs. Mix until creamy. Add the oil, kahlua and vodka; mix by hand until there are no lumps. Pour into a well-oiled bundt pan (8-cup size) and bake for approximately 45 minutes. Take it out of the oven and allow it to set a minute. Then flip it out onto the plate on which you intend to serve it. While still piping hot, open the can of store-bought chocolate fudge icing and spread it on the cake. It will melt into the cake and the result is celestial.

Apricot Rum Puffs

Makes 24 puffs

2 c. chopped dried apricots	1 c. chopped walnuts or pecans
2 c. dark seedless raisins	1 tsp. grated fresh lemon zest
3/4 c. water	1 T. fresh lemon juice
3/4 c. rum ☺	1 tsp. vanilla extract
2 T. butter	1 pkg. frozen puff pastry, thawed
2 3/4 tsp. cornstarch with 1 T. water	1 egg, beaten with 1 tsp. water

In a large saucepan, bring apricots, raisins, water, rum and butter to boil. Stir in cornstarch mixture and cook until thick. Remove from heat and stir in walnuts, lemon zest, juice and vanilla. Cool completely.

Preheat oven to 375°. Roll puff pastry and cut into 3-inch squares. Put 1 teaspoon vanilla in each center. Moisten corners and gather corners into a four-corner puff. Press firmly to seal. Brush top with egg wash before baking. Bake for 25 to 30 minutes, or until golden and puffed.

Hint: These puffs may be frozen.

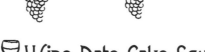

🍷 Wine Date Cake Squares

9x12-inch pan, about 24 pieces

1/4 c. shortening	1 tsp. cinnamon
1 c. brown sugar, firmly packed	1 tsp. nutmeg
1 egg	1 (8 oz.) pkg. pitted dates, cut up
1 1/2 c. sifted flour	1 c. coarsely-cut walnuts or pecans
1 tsp. baking soda	1 c. muscatel, port or sherry ☺
1/4 tsp. salt	

Cream shortening and sugar well. Add unbeaten egg and beat until blended. Mix and sift flour, baking soda, salt and spices. Add dates and nuts. Alternately add flour mixture and wine, beating well. Turn into greased and floured pan. Bake 30 minutes at 350°. Cool slightly before cutting. Sprinkle with powdered sugar, if you like.

🍷 Strawberry Portcake

4 servings

2 c. fresh strawberries, sliced	2 tsp. water
1/2 c. red currant or raspberry jelly	2 tsp. lemon juice
1/4 c. California port ☺	4 individual biscuit or sponge
1/2 tsp. grated orange rind	shortcakes
1 1/2 tsp. cornstarch	

Combine jelly, port and orange rind; heat slowly until jelly is melted. Stir cornstarch into water; add to jelly-port mixture. Cook and stir until sauce boils and becomes clear and thickened. Stir in lemon juice and remove from heat. Cool a few minutes, then add berries and spoon warm sauce over split shortcakes. You may top each serving with sour cream, whipped cream or vanilla ice cream.

Cherry Sabayon

8 servings

6 lg. egg yolks
1/3 c. sugar
1/3 c. dry white wine ☺
2 T. Grand Marnier ☺

1/2 pt. whipping cream, whipped
2 1/2 c. tart red cherries, fresh or
  frozen

In the top of a double boiler, combine the egg yolks and sugar, beating well. Add the wine to the egg mixture. Have the water in the double boiler simmering, and place the pan with the egg mixture on top. Whisk the mixture constantly until it thickens into a fluffy custard, about 5 minutes. Remove the egg mixture from the heat and beat until cool. Fold the stiffly-beaten whipped cream into the cooled egg mixture and add the Grand Marnier. Spoon the mixture over the cherries and serve.

Almond Sherry Pralines

2 dozen

3 c. light brown sugar
1 c. milk
1/2 tsp. grated orange rind
1/2 c. sherry ☺

2 T. butter
1/8 tsp. salt
1 c. halves of blanched almonds

Bring sugar and milk to boil in heavy saucepan, stirring until boiling point is reached. Add orange rind and sherry, stir until mixture again comes to a boil, then cook without stirring to soft ball stage, 240°. Add butter, salt and nuts; cool to lukewarm without stirring. Beat until creamy, then drop from spoon onto waxed paper. Wrap each praline in waxed paper, or better, transparent plastic.

♟ Cranberry Conserve

2 1/2 cups

1 (12 oz.) pkg. fresh cranberries
1/2 c. golden raisins
1/2 c. sugar

1/4 c. water
1/3 c. pear schnapps ☺

Preheat oven to 300° to 325°. In a 9x13-inch baking dish, combine all ingredients, except schnapps. Cover with foil. Bake 45 minutes. Remove foil and sprinkle schnapps on top. Cool.
Can be made ahead.

♟ Marvelous Melon

5 to 6 servings

1 c. blueberries
1 c. raspberries
2 c. sm. cantaloupe balls

1/3 c. shredded coconut
3 T. coconut liqueur ☺

Combine blueberries, raspberries, melon, coconut and coconut liqueur. Mix well. Refrigerate for several hours before serving.
Variation: Substitute for 1 cup cantaloupe, 1 cup of another in-season melon.

Apple Soufflé

8 servings

2 lb. tart green apples, cored &
  peeled
1/2 c. Riesling or slightly-sweet
  wine ☺
1/2 c. water
1/2 c. + 4 T. sugar, divided
Grated zest of 1 lemon
4 T. unsalted butter

4 oz. sliced leftover bread, no crust
1 egg
3/4 c. milk
1/2 tsp. vanilla extract
3/4 tsp. ground cinnamon, divided
2/3 c. raisins
2 T. apricot jam

Place apples, wine, water, 1/2 cup plus 2 tablespoons sugar and lemon zest in a medium-size heavy saucepan. Cook, covered, over medium heat, stirring occasionally until texture of applesauce, about 25 to 30 minutes.

Preheat oven to 350°. Butter a 2-quart soufflé dish. Butter bread on both sides and toast on a baking sheet until lightly toasted. Transfer to a large flat dish. Mix the egg, milk, vanilla, 2 tablespoons sugar and 1/4 teaspoon of cinnamon, and pour over the bread. Let stand about 30 minutes. Place raisins in a small bowl and add boiling water to cover. Let stand 15 minutes. Drain and pat dry. Add raisins, apricot jam and remaining 1/2 teaspoon cinnamon to the applesauce and stir thoroughly.

Line bottom and sides of prepared soufflé dish with bread. Pour apple mixture into dish and smooth top. Trim bread so it is even with the apple mixture. Bake about 45 minutes, or until set and light brown on top. Unmold and serve hot or warm.

Fruit Medley with Port

6 servings

Try this recipe with fruit variations, such as Royal Anne cherries or canned figs in place of apricots.

6 canned pear halves
6 canned peach halves
6 canned whole apricots
1 1/2 c. sugar
3/4 c. syrup from canned fruit

3/4 c. port ☺
1 1/2 tsp. grated orange rind
1 1/2 tsp. grated lemon rind
1 T. lemon juice

Drain fruit. Arrange 1 pear half, 1 peach half and 1 apricot in each of 6 dessert dishes. Combine remaining ingredients in a saucepan; bring to a boil, stirring until sugar is dissolved. Simmer 15 minutes. Let cool. Pour cooled syrup over fruit, and chill in the refrigerator for several hours before serving.

Put fresh strawberries chilled in ruby or
white port in a champagne or martini glass.

May Wine Berry Mold

6 servings

1 T. unflavored gelatin
1 (7 oz.) btl. sparkling water
1 c. May wine ☺
3 T. sugar

1 pt. fresh raspberries or
  strawberries
1 (3 oz.) pkg. cream cheese

   Soften gelatin in 1/4 cup sparkling water. Dissolve over boiling water. Mix with remaining water and wine. Add sugar. Chill until partially thickened. Fold half of berries into half of gelatin and turn into individual molds. Chill. Beat cheese with electric mixer until smooth. Add remaining gelatin and beat until blended. Pour over first layer and chill until firm. When ready to serve, unmold and garnish with remaining berries.

Strawberry Macaroon Whip

6 portions

1 pt. strawberries, sliced & lightly
  sugared
3 T. port ☺

2 c. coarse macaroon crumbs
1 c. heavy cream, whipped

   Sprinkle wine on macaroon crumbs and let stand for 30 minutes. Fold berries, crumbs and cream together and pile in sherbet dishes.

♟ Sherry Chiffon Pie

9-inch pie, 6 pieces

This is an old recipe, and one of the best of its kind.

1 c. milk
1/2 c. sugar
3 eggs, separated
1/8 tsp. nutmeg
1/4 tsp. salt
1 1/2 T. unflavored gelatin
4 T. milk

1 c. sherry ☺
1 c. heavy cream, whipped
1/2 c. slivered toasted almonds
1/4 tsp. vanilla
Baked pastry shell or graham
 cracker crust

Combine milk and sugar in saucepan and bring to scalding. Stir a little of the hot milk mixture into the beaten yolks; add nutmeg and salt. Return to hot mixture and cook over low heat, stirring until mixture coats a spoon. Remove from heat and add the gelatin, which has been softened in the 4 tablespoons milk. Stir to dissolve. Stir in wine gradually. Chill until mixture begins to thicken. Fold in stiff beaten egg whites, then fold in half of the whipped cream. Turn into pie shell and chill until firm. Top with remaining whipped cream flavored with vanilla. Sprinkle toasted almonds on top of whipped cream.

215

Notes & Recipes

INDEX

APPETIZERS

Hot Crab Souffle...1
Hot Crabmeat Dip..1
Sherried Tuna Pimiento Dip...2
Pickled Shrimp 2
Crab and Salmon Ring 3
Stuffed Clams 4
Holiday Cheese Bowl 5
Brie and Bourbon 6
Stuffed Edam Cheese...6
Chutney Party Pinwheels 7
Crab Puffs...8
Shrimp Bake...9
Shrimp Supreme...10
Sesame Chicken Kabobs..10
Sesame Chicken Wings 11
Wings for a Party...12
Artichoke Clam Puffs 12
Salmon Paté..13
Chicken Liver Paté..14
Chicken Livers En Brochette 15
Sherry Cheese Paté..15
Mushroom Flambé..16
Liver Paté..17
Mushroom Chicken Liver Paté 17
Meatball Stroganoff 18
Meatballs with Wine..19
Grilled Beef Strips 20
Swiss Cheese Fondue 20
Beef Tenderloin with Béarnaise Mayonnaise............21
Brie, Roquefort and Wild Mushroom Fondue............22
Chicken Fondue in Ginger Broth............................23-24

VEGGIES & SALADS

Squash and Zucchini Casserole 25
Creamed Squash Au Gratin..26
Bourbon Sweet Potatoes...27
Scalloped Mushrooms 27
Baked Bell Peppers with Tomatoes 28
Ham and Sweet Potato Casserole 29
Mustard Mushrooms...29
Mushrooms in Cognac Herb Sauce 30
Southwestern Chili Beans 31
Sugar Snaps and Mushrooms...32
Elegant Spinach 33
Green Beans with Mint...34
Wild Rice Forestiere..35
Carrots Cointreau..36
Carrots with White Grapes...36
Squash Risotto 37
Rice with Spinach and Feta Cheese 38
German Red Cabbage..39
Almond Wild Rice 40
Molded Melon Ball Salad...41
Party Cherry Mold 42
Potato Salad with White Wine 43
Shrimp Salad with Wine, in Tomatoes 44
Avocado, Bacon and Chicken Salad...45
Grilled Breast of Chicken Salad 46
Seafood Mousse Louise...47
Avocado-Lime Mousse..48
Deviled Eggs 48
Hot Potato Salad with Wine 49
Steak and Spinach with Hot Pan Dressing......................................50

SEAFOOD

Brazilian Stuffed Whitefish...51
Tilapia with Lime Caper Sauce 52
Teriyaki Swordfish...53
Spicy Swordfish with Tomato and Orange Sauce............54
Shrimp-Stuffed Trout 55
Trout Marguery..56
Grilled Salmon with Mustard Dill Sauce..........................57
Seared Salmon with Orange Glaze....................................58
Herb-Crusted Salmon with Sun-Dried Tomato Sauce 59
Easy Herbed Grilled Salmon..60
Broiled Pompano...61
Filet of Sole 62
Tuna Steaks in Marinade 63
Peppered Ahi Tuna with Mushrooms and Port Wine......64
Fresh Clams with Artichokes and Tomatoes 65-66
Lobster with Red Wine Risotto 67-68
Lobster Thermidor 69
Decadant Lobster and Vodka Sauce..................................70
Lobster Thermidor 71
Savory Deviled Crabs...72
Sherried Crabmeat 73
Crab Cake with Mustard Sauce 74
Panned Oysters..75
Mussels Marinière...76
Oysters and Crab...77
Coquilles St. Jacques...78
Scallops and Shrimp in White Wine Sauce 79
Broiled Shrimp with White Wine 80
Shrimp Scampi 80
Baked Stuffed Shrimp...81
Prawns Sambeau Flambé...82

Seafood Risotto 83
Shrimp with Wild Rice 84
Special Shrimp Curry 85
Shrimp A La Mann 86
Shrimp in Tomato Cream Sauce 87
Seafood Supreme 88

POULTRY

Fruit-Glazed Roast Chicken 89
Chicken Breasts with Ginger 90
Chicken Cacciatora 91
Chicken Marengo 92
Hawaiian Chicken for a Party 93
Peruvian Chicken 94
Arroz Con Pollo 95
Chicken Flambé with Brandied Cherry Sauce 96
Chicken Baked in Foil 97
Chicken Pie 98
Coq au Vin 99
Vermouth Chicken Scallopine 100
Chicken Stir Fry 101
Chicken Breasts with Leeks and Pine Nuts
     (Can also use Pork Chops or Pork Tenderloin) 102
Easy Chicken Piccata 103
Gruyére and Chicken Roulade 104
Quick Couscous with Chicken 105
Chicken and Vermouth, Mushrooms and Onions 106
Chicken 'N Potato Bake 107
Chicken, Sausage and Black Olives 108
Chicken Cacciatore 109-110
Chicken with Red Wine and Mustard 111-112

Chicken and Ham Imperial 113
Creamy Chicken Marsala..114
Southwestern Shepherd's Pie.. 115-116
Cornish Hens with Apricot, Port and Balsamic Sauce 117
Rock Cornish Hens with Burgundy Wine.............................118
Sherried Turkey with Grapes...119
Turkey Scalloppini with Capers and Lemon 120
Baked Turkey Sandwiches...121
Turkey Timbales with Mushroom Wine Sauce 122
Bourbon Chicken or Turkey 123

MEATS
BEEF-PORK-LAMB

Châteaubriand...125
Brainless Beef Sherry 125
Beef Filet with Peppercorns and Chutney....................................126
Burgundy Pot Roast...127
Lobster - Stuffed Tenderloin of Beef 128-129
Beef Tenderloin in Mushroom Port Sauce..130
Pan-Roasted Beef Tenderloin with Rosemary and Garlic.............131
Sautéed Filet Mignon...132
Beef in Herb Wine Sauce..133
Green Pepper Steak...134
Steak Diane 135-136
Boeuf Bourguignon...136
Steaks with Red Wine Sauce...137
Steak au Poivre 138-139
Brisket Braised in White Wine 140
Beef Short Ribs Braised with Citrus 141-142
Easy Wine-Marinated Brisket..143
Stringed Beef Brisket...144

Slow Cooker Burgundy Meat Loaf..145
Beef Brisket with Carmelized Onions and Wine Sauce.......... 146-147
Marinated Hamburgers...148
Potatoed Pork Loin 148
Pork Tenderloin in Dijon Sauce 149
Roast Pork with Apricot Demi-Glace....................................... 150-151
Barbecued Pork Tenderloin...151
Spareribs, Apples and Sauerkraut..152
Rum Roasted Pork 153-154
Teriyaki Pork Tenderloin...154
Pork Tenderloins Braised with Red Cabbage 155
Veal Scallopine with Mushroom and
    Sun-Dried Tomato Cream Sauce 156
Stuffed Breast of Veal with Wild Rice...157
Rack of Lamb with Fig and Port Wine Sauce.................................158
Lamb Sausages with Red Cabbage..159
Braised Lamb Shanks 160
Roast Leg of Lam With Rosemary 161
Braised Lamb Shanks with Sour Cream and Capers.....................162
Veal Scallopine Alla Marsala...163
Leg of Lamb with Artichoke Stuffing 164
Castilian Veal..165
Stuffed Veal Chops Chablis..166
Quick Osso Buco 167
Roast Goose with Oranges and Madeira................................. 168-169

SOUPS, STEWS, SAUCES,
MARINADES & MISCELLANEOUS

She-Crab Soup 171
Shrimp Bisque..171
Shrimp and Scallop Stew 172
Seafood Pasta Chowder 173

Bouillabaisse 174
Onion Soup 175
Cheddar and Bacon Soup 176
Orange Carrot Bisque 177
Fresh Mushroom Soup 178
Black Bean Soup 179
Potato Soup with Wine..180
Sun-Dried Tomatoes Beef Stew...180
Parsley Soup 181
Chicken Stew in White Wine...182
Beef Stew 183
Beef Stew 184
Sun-Dried Tomato Spaghetti Sauce..185
Red or White Wine Marinade 186
Béarnaise Sauce 187
Hollandaise Sauce 187
Barbecue Sauce 188
Beurre Blanc..189
Peach Sauce...190
Raspberry Sauce..190
Sherried French Toast...191
Scrambled Eggs with Chablis...191
Swiss Cheese Pie 192
Cheddar Cheese Spread with Port 193
Brainless French Bread...193

DESSERTS

Glazed Bananas 195
Strawberry Amaretto...195
Peach, Honey and Cardamom Wine Cordial 196
Sherried Baked Cranberry Sauce...196
Baked Apples Marsala...197

Glazed Oranges in Cointreau 198
Flaming Bananas 199
Hot Fruit Compote 200
Lazy Daisy Cake 201
Bread Pudding with Whiskey Cream 202-203
Eggnog Refrigerator Cake 204
Glazed Strawberry Pie 205
Pork Wine Cake 205
Jellied Cherries or Peaches in Port 206
Wine Baked Peaches 206
Vodka Puddin Cake 207
Apricot Rum Puffs 208
Wine Date Cake Squares 209
Strawberry Portcake 209
Cherry Sabayon 210
Almond Sherry Pralines 210
Cranberry Conserve 211
Marvelous Melon 211
Apple Soufflé 212
Fruit Medley with Port 213
May Wine Berry Mold 214
Strawberry Macaroon Whip 214
Sherry Chiffon Pie 215

Converting to Metric Measurements

MEASURES:

English	Metric
1/4 tsp.	1 ml
1/2 tsp.	2 ml
1 tsp.	5 ml
1 tbsp.	15 ml
2 tbsp.	25 ml
1/4 cup	50 ml
1/3 cup	75 ml
1/2 cup	125 ml
2/3 cup	150 ml
3/4 cup	175 ml
1 cup	250 ml
1 1/2 cups	375 ml
2 cups	500 ml

WEIGHTS

For fish, meat, poultry and bulk fruits and vegetables

English	Metric
1 lb.	500 g
3/4 lb. or 12 oz.	375 g
1/2 lb. or 8 oz.	250 g
1/4 lb. or 4 oz.	125 g

OVEN TEMPERATURES

Fahrenheit	Celsius
300°	150°
325°	160°
350°	180°
375°	190°
400°	200°
425°	220°
450°	230°

DEEP-FAT FRYING TEMPERATURES

Fahrenheit	Celsius
350°	170°
375°	190°
385°	195°
395°	200°

CANDY-MAKING TEMPERATURES

Stage	Celsius (Fahrenheit)
Thread Stage	110°-112° C. (230°-234° F.)
Soft-Ball Stage	112°-115° C. (234°-240° F.)
Firm-Ball Stage	118°-120° C. (244°-248° F.)
Hard-Ball Stage	121°-130° C. (250°-266° F.)
Soft-Crack Stage	132°-143° C. (270°-290° F.)
Hard-Crack Stage	149°-154° C. (300°-310° F.)

PAN SIZES

Inches	Centi-meters	Capacity (Liters)
Rectangular		
10 x 6 x 1 1/2	25 x 15 x 4	1.5
11 x 7 x 1 1/2	28 x 18 x 4	1.8
12 x 7 1/2 x 2	30 x 19 x 5	2.5
13 x 9 x 2	33 x 23 x 5	3.5
Square		
8 x 8 x 2	20 x 20 x 5	1.8
9 x 9 x 2	23 x 23 x 5	2.4
Round		
8 x 1 1/2	20 x 4	1.2
9 x 1 1/2	23 x 4	1.5
Tube		
9-inch	23 x 9	2.7
10-inch	25 x 10	3.1
Jelly Roll		
15 x 10 x 1	39 x 27 x 25	
Loaf		
8 x 4 x 2	22 x 11 x 6	1.5
9 x 5 x 3	23 x 13 x 8	2.0
Pie Pans		
4 1/4-inch	11 x 3	
9-inch	23 x 3	
10-inch	25 x 4	